"Dr. Mark Baker marries faith and mode[...]
tain to open both the mind and soul. His [...]
in science and undeniably imbued with C[...]

Doug Richardson
Screenwriter and novelist; movies include
Die Hard 2, *Bad Boys*, and *Welcome to Mooseport*

"*Overcoming Shame* is a great read written by an experienced psychotherapist. Dr. Baker draws on many concepts from Scripture and positive psychology—humility, mercy, forgiveness, compassion, and love, to name a few. This book will lift your head, lift your spirits, and lift your eyes toward Jesus."

Everett L. Worthington, Jr, PhD
Professor of psychology, Virginia Commonwealth University
Author of 30+ books on forgiveness and related areas
including *Heroic Humility* (with Scott Allison)

"If left unchecked, shame becomes a malignant cancer that extends itself from personal pain to potential violence to self and others. Dr. Baker not only rigorously addresses the destructive power of shame, but he also provides the only guaranteed step-by-step process for being eternally healed from this progressive source of internal and external life-threatening hurt and pain. The timing is right for Dr. Baker's exceptionally well-written book *Overcoming Shame*. This book is a must-read, a solution for a time such as this."

Mack Harnden, PhD
Clinical psychologist, founder and
president of the Forgiveness Institute

"Though shame is seldom discussed in churches, it's an emotion that all Christians deal with—most often poorly. We tend to deny or ignore it, which doesn't work and in turn causes more humiliation and pushes us further on the downward spiral of shame. Thankfully, Christian psychologist Mark Baker explains a better way. Rich in detail and depth, *Overcoming Shame* will also help people deal with guilt, resentment, envy, jealousy, and even narcissism. I know of no one who couldn't benefit from this insightful book, and I especially recommend it to pastors and other church leaders in order to help people defeat a problem that has destroyed individuals, families, and communities since, well, we emerged from Eden."

RICK STEDMAN
Pastor and author of
31 Surprising Reasons to Believe in God

Dr. Mark W. Baker

overcoming
shame

HARVEST HOUSE PUBLISHERS
EUGENE, OREGON

Cover by Jason Gabbert Design

Cover photos © Rocket Photos, Slippazz / shutterstock

Published in association with Hartline Literary Agency, LLC, of 123 Queenston Drive, Pittsburgh, PA 15235.

The examples used in this book are composites of real-life stories and no example is intended to represent any one particular individual. In addition, all people's names and details of their situations have been changed in order to protect their privacy.

OVERCOMING SHAME
Copyright © 2018 Mark W. Baker
Published by Harvest House Publishers
Eugene, Oregon 97408
www.harvesthousepublishers.com

ISBN 978-0-7369-7130-0 (pbk.)
ISBN 978-0-7369-7131-7 (eBook)

Printed in the United States of America

18 19 20 21 22 23 24 25 26 / BP-SK / 10 9 8 7 6 5 4 3 2 1

ACKNOWLEDGMENTS

It takes a village to write a book. Every idea captured in these pages is the result of many hours of conversation, correspondence, prayer, and time spent with people who have influenced me in so many ways that I will never be able to recount them all. I am thankful for the years Dr. Robert Stolorow mentored me while Dr. Howard Bacal kept me sane. I am grateful for my friends and colleagues at the La Vie Christian Counseling Center for collaborating with me for decades in the care of our patients, and keeping me honest in our weekly consultations. The personal support of Dr. Mack Harnden, Dr. Scott Weimer, Dr. Don Morgan, James David Hinton, Dwight Case, and Eugene Lowe have made my professional life possible. And this book would not even exist if were not for the dedication of Jim Hart of Hartline Literary Agency and the wisdom of Terry Glaspey of Harvest House Publishers. But most importantly, I thank God daily for blessing me with my wife, Barbara, and my amazing children, Brendan, Aidan, and Brianna. They make it all worthwhile.

Contents

INTRODUCTION:

What God's Grace
Can Do for You

S hame. Everybody feels it, but nobody wants to talk about it. Because no one's life has been perfect, everyone has feelings of shame—just to a different degree. I would like to invite you to go on a journey of discovery with me. This journey is not to some distant place. The journey we are about to take is inward, inside of you. That is where shame hides, and that is where we need to go to bring it out into the light of day so that you can be healed of it.

Fortunately, you and I can take this journey of self-discovery in the privacy of your own home, or backyard, or wherever you like to go to read books. You don't have to come to my psychotherapy office, attend a conference, or even let anyone know you are about to explore your shame. That should make your exploration a little easier. But it does require courage on your part. Admitting you have feelings of shame is not an easy thing, so I applaud your courage for picking up this book. Over many years, I have worked with countless people who have been greatly helped by having the courage to admit to their feelings of shame; and their ability to be vulnerable enough to ask for help has paid off. They have been richly rewarded for taking similar journeys with me, so I have an idea that you are about to receive some benefit for your efforts as well.

In my work as a psychologist, I have found that chronic feelings of shame have caused more problems for the average person than any other feeling out there. The good news is that ongoing feelings of shame are only a problem if you never address them, and you just took the first step toward doing something about that. Now I'll do my best to help you get to the root of any problems you may have with shame and show you how to overcome them.

God made us with the capacity to feel shame for a good reason, and he has not abandoned us to a life of painful feelings without help. Thankfully, he sent his Son as an example of how to live well. You and I can benefit from the life of the only person ever to have walked this earth shame-free. He showed us how the grace of God can overcome anything in this life and how it can overcome any feelings of shame in yours.

> Let us run with perseverance the race marked out for us, fixing our eyes on Jesus, the pioneer and perfecter of faith. For the joy set before him he endured the cross, scorning its shame, and sat down at the right hand of the throne of God.
>
> **HEBREWS 12:1-2**

CHAPTER ONE

Do You Have a Problem with Guilt or Shame?

I feel really bad," Ethan confessed, looking down.

"Okay," I responded, trying not to interrupt what he was struggling to say.

"I mean, I think I'm a good person—*aren't I?*" he said, looking up at me.

I gave him a slight smile, encouraging him to go on. I could tell this wasn't actually a question, but more like he was pleading with me to talk him out of what he had already concluded—that he *wasn't* a good person.

"You know me. I'm a 'by the book' kind of guy," Ethan continued. "I follow the rules, and I expect others to do the same. That's the only way you can get respect these days. Our world is so out of control; it's just crazy out there. I've provided for my family and always tried to do the right thing. Well, until now, I guess. I don't know...I mean, I don't know how this happened. I feel so bad."

Actually, Ethan *was* a pretty good person. I had come to know him well since he started therapy with me. He originally called me for help because his wife had discovered some e-mail messages between him and a woman at work. She was a colleague, one whom he respected and considered a friend, a good friend. At first they found themselves talking about work, and both felt supported by how much they had in common and the perspectives they shared. Then, over time, their conversations became more personal. They started sharing feelings about other people at work, friends they had in common, and eventually about their marriages. This became a slippery slope into even more intimate conversations that they weren't having at home with their spouses. Now they were saying things to each other that were far too intimate for just friends. Without realizing it, Ethan had fallen into an emotional affair. It wasn't something he was looking for. It just happened.

The most common place for affairs to start is at work. Most people don't see affairs coming because in most situations they think they are just talking to a friend. But if a person isn't careful, *just friends* can change into something more than that very easily.[1] And since Ethan's wife had gotten involved, he had been struggling to figure out just how he felt about everything—especially himself.

Ethan was confused just as most people are confused about how they should feel when they do hurtful things. Was he feeling guilt for what he had done, or was he ashamed of himself? Often we use the terms interchangeably, so that makes the dilemma even more confusing. All he knew is that he felt bad, and he had come to me to help him sort out his feelings.

GUILT OR SHAME?

Guilt and shame are not the same. Guilt is the bad feeling you have for having gone too far. You did something you should not have done, and now you regret it. Shame is the feeling you get for not going far enough. You feel regret for being inadequate. Guilt is about what you *did*; shame is about who you *are*. Both are bad feelings, but knowing the difference is imperative.[2]

If you never felt any guilt or shame, you would be what psychologists call a *psychopath*—a person with no conscience. Psychopaths don't feel bad about anything they do, and they never feel bad about themselves despite the horrible things they are capable of doing. We don't know exactly what causes psychopathy, but you don't want it—trust me. I've been to a maximum security prison and talked to psychopaths. There are some very bad people on the planet, but ironically the reason they are so bad is because they never question their badness. If you feel guilt and shame, you should be grateful. At least you are not a psychopath.

The Bible has a lot to say about guilt. Mostly guilt feels bad, but it exists to help us. Paul talks about a "godly sorrow" that leads people to repentance and produces good things in their lives (2 Corinthians 7:11). So guilt is a useful antipsychopathic tool for normal folks. What I call *healthy guilt* is the capacity to feel bad when you have hurt someone else, God, or even yourself. Healthy guilt is motivated by love. You want to be a good person, and if you hurt someone, your healthy guilt stimulates you to do the loving thing. In most cases, you take action to make amends for what you did wrong. Guilt comes from *doing* something wrong, so it is corrected by you *doing* something right. Healthy guilt motivates you to do the right thing to restore damaged relationships. It comes from having a conscience, and that in itself is a good thing. God created guilt to guide us toward restoring our relationships with him, but it works as a guide for restoring relationships with one another as well.

Not all guilt is productive. I call this kind *neurotic guilt*. It is not motivated by love and is rooted in underlying shame. Neurotic guilt is not about making amends or figuring out the loving thing to do to make things right in your relationships. Neurotic guilt is about self-preservation and the fear of getting caught. If your guilt is focused on you taking care of yourself, it rarely produces anything good. Sure, you feel bad because of something you did, but you are not really motivated by your love of God or others to make things right with them. You are more concerned about being exposed and getting in trouble. Neurotic guilt is better than being a psychopath, but it's not really about making things right with others because its real motivation is to cover over painful feelings of shame that you don't want anyone to see. In other words, neurotic guilt is about saving your own skin.

Sadly, neurotic guilt is pretty popular. Because we were designed by God to feel guilt, we all have the capacity for it. It's just that sometimes we are not clear about its underlying motivation. Do you feel bad because you have hurt someone and want to bring your offense out into the open for healing even if you have to risk looking foolish? Or do you feel bad about something that happened and hope no one will ever bring it up again? If the fear of getting caught wins out, you are suffering from neurotic guilt, and it is likely to be with you for a long time. Neurotic guilt lasts, sometimes for a lifetime, exactly *because* we don't want to talk about it. Or if we do, we never get to the root of the problem to restore relationships in any meaningful way.

I'm going to talk about forgiveness later, which is the best solution for guilt, but I'll just say at this point that neurotic guilt isn't really about seeking forgiveness; rather, it is a form of self-punishment that substitutes for restored relationships and keeps people stuck. If you think you can solve your problems with guilt all by yourself (by punishing yourself with neurotic guilt), you are likely to be wrestling with your bad feelings for a very long time.

Shame feels bad too. But it is different from guilt. Shame is the painful feeling of disconnection from others that comes from feeling defective. You may think you feel bad because of things you have done (and can give anyone a long list of screwups that you are ready to confess if you need to), but the truth is that shame is a bad feeling you have about yourself, and you had that feeling long before you committed any of the things you think caused it. In fact, your shame is probably *the reason* you did the things you did wrong in the first place. Feeling shame makes you feel bad about yourself for being who you are and thus predisposes you to act in bad ways. So as you can see, getting a grip on your shame becomes pretty important. Shame is a deeper and more toxic problem than your guilt, and one that needs your attention. I say "your" here because we all feel shame, at least to some degree.

So what was going on with Ethan? Did he feel guilty, or was he dealing with shame? Well, mostly it was guilt. Ethan didn't have as big a problem with his self-worth as he did with *bad boundaries*. And failing to maintain boundaries is a major culprit when it comes to affairs at work. It is true that Ethan's hidden feelings of shame (hidden from him anyway) did cause him to need the attention of an attractive woman at work, and the compensatory need for this type of affirmation was part of what was going on. But the biggest problem Ethan had was that he had hurt the woman he loved more than anyone in the world, and he felt terrible about that. He never stopped to ask himself when he was flirting with his colleague, "How much would it hurt my wife if she heard me saying this right now?"

His actions were very selfish, and it was going to take years to repair the damage he caused, but Ethan truly felt bad for hurting his wife, not just because he got caught doing it. He didn't blame his actions on her with things like "Well, if I got a little more attention at home, I wouldn't need to look elsewhere" or try to wiggle out of his hurtful behavior in any way. He was wrong, and he could see that now. He learned the hard truth that it takes years to build up trust with someone, but you can lose it in an instant if you are not careful. I believe Ethan is basically a good man and is going to do what it takes to regain the trust he lost with his wife. I believe this because his godly sorrow is directing him to do it. If his biggest issue was with shame, well then, that would be a different story.

THE DEAFENING SILENCE OF SHAME

One of the things that makes shame so difficult to deal with is silence. By its very nature, shame seeks to hide itself, and us with it. Some people love to talk about their guilt, as if to elicit our sympathy either to reassure them that they are not bad people or to confirm for them that they should feel bad, and that they are not wrong for feeling that way. But shame is different. Even though some people want to talk about having done bad things, no one wants to talk about being a bad person. Shame motivates us to want to keep secrets. And the toxic power of shame only grows stronger in the dark.

Many years ago I was invited to preview the movie *The Prince of Tides* before it was released in the theaters. Barbra Streisand directed the movie and asked me to give her my opinion of it as a psychologist. The movie is about a psychiatrist, played by Streisand, who has a suicidal patient who has no memories of her childhood, so the psychiatrist develops a relationship with her patient's brother, played by Nick Nolte, to try to find out what happened to her. I didn't like that the psychiatrist became involved in an affair with her patient's brother, but I did like the movie.

I will never forget sitting there in the theater watching as Streisand and Nolte acted out the effects of childhood sexual abuse on adult survivors in her psychotherapy office. In his Oscar-nominated performance, Nolte skillfully depicts a repressed southern gentleman with a failing marriage and an inability to connect intimately to anyone, even his own daughters who obviously love him. He describes himself as "the champion of keeping secrets," but in his attempt to help his hospitalized sister, he finds himself opening up to her therapist. He begrudgingly admits to Streisand's character, "For a man who never talked, I was doing nothing else."

In one gripping scene, Nolte's character reveals for the first time ever that he, his sister, and their mother were all raped by escaped convicts who broke into their home one rainy night when their father was away. His now-deceased older brother came in with a shotgun and killed two of them while his mother stabbed the third to death in the back.

"I'm surprised you and Savannah survived at all. You were just a boy. What happened after that? How did your family deal with it?" Streisand asks.

"We didn't tell anyone," Nolte whispers.

"You didn't tell anyone? Not even the police?" she responds incredulously.

"Mama said, 'It's over. Take these carcasses outside and clean this mess up,'" Nolte continues, as if in a trance.

He says his mother just kept repeating, "This did not happen. This did not happen," over and over again. She threatened to disown any of the children who breathed a word about the event to anyone. They buried the bodies outside and never mentioned it again, not even to their father, who came home later for a family meal with them. Then, Nolte utters one of the most profound statements about sexual abuse that I have ever heard in a movie. With an almost expressionless face, he says, "We sat around and ate as if nothing was wrong. God help me. I think the silence was worse than the rape."

Three days later, his sister tried to kill herself for the first time. All Nolte's character can say about that is, "She could keep quiet. But she couldn't lie."[3]

Here I was sitting in a special movie theater, two seats away from Blythe Danner with her skinny (at that time unknown) teenage daughter between us, named Gwyneth Paltrow, doing my best to try to act professional, but I was fighting back a tear forming in the corner of my eye as I grasped the profound nature of Nolte's words. Streisand's direction of the film cut straight to the heart of the disastrous relationship between silence and shame. The tragedy of childhood molestation and rape is that the victim has done nothing wrong. But so often the perpetrator feels no guilt, so the victim is left to try to make sense out of a senseless act of violence to the human psyche.

Some trauma specialists call this the *transfer of guilt*, because the person who should feel guilty doesn't, so the guilt is transferred to the victim instead. But I think it is worse than that. When something as horrible as rape happens to someone who is powerless and who didn't *do* anything wrong, that person is left with the shame of feeling that they *are* something wrong. If you are treated as though you are a worthless "piece of meat" (as one of the convicts in the movie actually said), you come away with the belief that you are. The real damage done to victims of molestation and rape is not just guilt but soul-crushing shame. All trauma experts will tell you that the worst thing you can do to victims of this type of crime is to tell them never to speak about it. They often feel just as Nolte said, that *the silence is worse than the rape*, because the damaging effects of the rape are not only perpetuated for years without anything changing, but they actually get worse, as we saw depicted in Nolte's suicidal sister's inability to function in life.

Streisand goes on to have Nolte's character open up his feelings about the trauma, breaking a lifetime of silence for him. His character is not only transformed by this shattering of silence but is able to facilitate his sister's healing through emotional honesty and to return to a life of sanity as well.

Once shame gets its claws in us, silence only makes it worse. Shame disconnects us from others and causes us to doubt our worth, as if we don't have anything of value to offer others. This lie is perpetuated by silence, and it can be exposed as false only through having the courage to speak honestly about how we feel to others who will listen. Our fear is that our worthlessness will only be confirmed if we open up to others, but the irony is that only by opening up to others can the toxic power of shame be dispelled.

The psalmist tells us that we are "fearfully and wonderfully made" (Psalm 139:14). This is the truth about us. Shame is based on the lie that this is not true, and that our worthlessness disqualifies us from the right to connect with God and others. Believing this lie leaves us feeling profoundly alone and incapable of the intimacy for which we were designed. Marital difficulties, family troubles, psychological problems, workplace relationship conflicts, authority clashes, and multiple other tragic effects will follow. Your own doubt about your self-worth is one of the greatest sources of dysfunction in your life, and refusing to keep silent about the sources of your shame is one of the most significant things you can do to help you be the person God created you to be.

Guilt as a Defense Against Shame

As you can see, shame is more difficult to deal with than guilt. Guilt is something you can speak about, confess, and even manage if you know how. Thankfully, God has given us the wonderful tool of forgiveness and has spelled out for us in the Bible how it works. Shame, however, is more challenging. No one wants to feel it, speak about it, or even believe they have a problem with it. So what do some people do as an alternative? They try to pretend that they feel guilty instead. Cute trick, if it worked.

Olivia came to therapy because of the problems she was having in her marriage. Relationship difficulties are one of the most common reasons people seek out therapy. Our relationships are valuable to us, so when things are not going well, we are wise not only to seek help from a marriage counselor but to look at ourselves to see how we can do things better on our end. Individual psychotherapy is a great resource for people today, and smart people take advantage of great resources.

Olivia is bright and insightful, and she has always been a thoughtful person who tries to take responsibility for herself and improve her situation whenever she can. She married early in life and now has a wonderful daughter with whom she has a good relationship. But over the years, her relationship with her husband has become increasingly dissatisfying for her. Because he has been successful in his career, she was able to stop working and devote herself to their daughter. They both felt this was a good thing for her to do, and she didn't have any complaints about this arrangement. But she was growing increasingly unhappy with the distance she felt in her marriage, and she wanted to get some perspective on how she could change to help make things better.

"I don't want to be negative, but I'm just not sure we are making any progress in our marital counseling," Olivia stated apologetically.

"Well, these things can take time. What are your concerns?" I asked.

"We go every week. We've been pretty good about that, but I still have this sense that something is just not right. I mean, he has become so secretive over the past several years. He must feel the distance that has grown between us, but every time I ask him how things are going, I always get the same answer: 'Fine.' *Really?* How can he believe things are *fine* when I'm not sure I even know what he's thinking half the time? It sure doesn't feel fine to me."

"You want more of a connection with him," I said.

"Exactly!" she responded quickly. "It's like I'm bugging him when

I try to talk about how I feel. You're a man. Do I seem like some nagging female to you?"

"You seem like a woman who needs to express herself to her husband and longs to have him respond in the same way with you," I said.

"Yes, that's it. I have a longing for more of an emotional connection with him. I just must not be doing it right." Then, somewhat hesitantly, she said, "I don't mean to be difficult or anything, but all this insight you are giving me is nice and everything, but really, *what should I do*? If I could only figure out what I'm doing wrong, I would change it. You can be honest with me; I can take it. Just tell me what I'm doing wrong."

This is a very common question that psychologists get—and we hate it. There is no good way to respond to the question "What should I do?" In Olivia's case, if I told her what to do, I am certain that she would go right out and do it. She doesn't have any difficulty with following instructions or problem solving. In fact, she is pretty good at it, as evidenced by her friends frequently seeking out her advice on things. So if I told her what to do, my counsel would probably confirm her suspicion that something was wrong with her for not being able to figure out a solution on her own. She didn't truly need my advice on what to do; a deeper problem was going on that we needed to work out.

After a number of sessions with Olivia pleading with me to tell her where she was wrong, I was able to get her to take the focus off of her performance in her marriage and place it on how she felt about herself. Eventually we were able to determine that this feeling of disconnection she had in her marriage was not new, and that she had felt this way pretty much all of her life. She was raised by a punitive, inconsistent mother and a distant father who failed to protect her from her mother's frequent outbursts of anger. She would hide in her room to avoid the conflict that her mother seemed to thrive on, and she never invited anyone over for fear of her mother doing something that would humiliate her in front of her friends. The result was that Olivia grew up feeling disconnected from almost everyone. She married her husband when she was only eighteen to escape the turmoil of her home life, and then she moved as far away as she could as the solution to that unsolvable problem. Her husband was a quiet, hardworking man, much like her father, and one she was convinced would never treat her as her mother had.

Over time Olivia came to see that she hadn't married her husband for an emotional connection; she married him because he was safe. Emotional connection was a luxury she had never considered at age eighteen. Olivia came to realize that when she got married, not only was her need for safety from abuse more important than emotional intimacy, but she didn't really believe that she actually deserved this type of deep connection. Olivia's greatest problem was not that she felt guilty for not knowing what to do about the lack of connection in her marriage; it was that she felt too ashamed to believe she was worth having emotional intimacy.

Often when people ask me what to do, I hesitate to respond because I'm not sure if they are trying to use guilt as a defense against shame. If you feel guilty for what you have or have not done, that is preferable to feeling shame for not being who you feel you should be. In Olivia's case, her shame was causing her to accept a level of disconnection that was dissatisfying on the one hand but strangely congruent with her feelings of worthlessness on the other. She had great advice and wonderful insight, but she had painful feelings of self-doubt that prevented her from being vulnerable and emotionally connecting in the ways she truly longed for.

Gradually I was able to witness Olivia overcome those feelings of shame that had been thwarting her connection to others throughout her life. As much as I would like to say that my brilliant insights are what cured her, Olivia and I know it wasn't as much those as it was the safe place we created for her to be vulnerable with me about her deepest longings and feelings. Shame was healed not through better performance but through vulnerably exposing shame's lie that Olivia wasn't worth being connected to. Once that lie was brought into the light, her shame of worthlessness gradually lost its grip on her. Then, quite naturally, her connection with her husband began to change—in subtle ways at first, but then more obviously as she became convinced that she had something of value to offer. She even was able to set boundaries with her mother that she had never felt entitled to do before, and she developed new relationships with others that were more satisfying emotionally and spiritually. And not surprisingly, she stopped asking me what she should do.

~

Both guilt and shame are strong emotions that you must acknowledge and deal with for your relationships to go well. To manage your guilt, you must *do* things differently. Being honest about wrongdoing, repenting of it, and seeking forgiveness are things you can do in response to your guilt. To deal with your shame, you must actually *be* different. That is, you must be vulnerable and experience what it is like to share feelings honestly with others in ways that change you. This type of emotional vulnerability creates an atmosphere where you can expose the lie that you are worthless and replace that lie with the truth that you are fearfully and wonderfully made. Many people do not even know they believe the lie in the first place. So being emotionally vulnerable is how we find it out.

Being vulnerable is not easy, especially when you have been hurt. Let's take a look at where shame comes from and what you need to know to deal with it.

CHAPTER TWO

What Causes Shame?

I must apologize for all the confusion out there regarding shame, including that caused by many of the things written by my fellow psychologists. Some authors think there are two kinds of shame, a healthy shame and an unhealthy one. Others believe there is absolutely no evidence to support any healthy benefits of shame whatsoever. Some psychologists are convinced that shame is learned over the course of our development; others believe it is innate. Some of the most famous psychological experts almost never talk about shame in their theories; others believe it is the central problem that explains most of human psychopathology. And, sadly, many writers don't make a clear distinction between guilt and shame, making it impossible for us to know if we are even talking about the same thing (which I think is the biggest explanation for all the confusion). Sorry about that.

First of all, Freud was wrong. I take a secret delight in being able to say this, because I am psychoanalytic in my theoretical orientation (remember, Freud started psychoanalysis), but most modern-day psychoanalysts don't agree with much of what Freud believed either. Freud thought humans were motivated by the instinctual drives of sex and aggression. We are not. Humans are motivated by emotions, which is how we connect in our relationships.[1] Quite different from what Freud thought, we are experiencing some form of these emotions from the very moment we are born.

We now know that infants are born into the world with an emerging sense of self that is hardwired to seek out relationships.[2] This nascent sense of self has physical reactions to the world (and the people in it) that cause infants to make certain evaluations of their world, which we call *affects*. These affects are then remembered in implicit memory, or the right hemisphere of the brain (the *feeling* part of the brain). When we develop the capacity to use language (in the left hemisphere of the brain) a few years later, we can put these affects into words, and that is what we typically call feelings—affects you can express with words. The technical distinction between affects, feelings, and emotions is not important (and of course, scientists don't all agree on the definitions), so I think it is okay to use the terms interchangeably. The key thing is to recognize that we are feeling *something* from the very moment of birth, and even before then, that motivates us to regulate ourselves and the relationships around us.

Shame is an emotion. The evidence to support the idea that it is inherited is pretty weak, but it does start very early. Researchers have measured relationship-seeking behavior in three-day-old infants, and if that relationship-seeking behavior is thwarted, infants respond negatively. Many researchers believe that early negative reaction is a primitive form of shame.[3] Infants can't feel bad about what they have done because that requires a higher form of cognitive development. In other words, guilt comes online later than shame. But infants can have a global sense of feeling bad about themselves.[4] They don't remember it as an event that is stored in the left hemisphere of the brain (the *rational* part of the brain) because the capacity for this level of thinking isn't developed yet. But we now know that they can remember it implicitly, as a feeling that has not yet been put into words. Infants can have a global sense that they lack the efficacy or agency to connect to the caregivers they were designed by God to seek out from birth. This painful feeling is the prototype of what we later come to identify more clearly as shame. If my life depends on connecting with you, and you don't respond in the way I need, I am very likely to get the feeling that I am just not worth your connection. This leads me to the feeling that something must be wrong with me, and I am now looking for somewhere to hide. That's shame.

So, some form of primitive shame starts to develop right from the start. If you are a parent, don't get too distressed yet. Not only is being perfectly attuned to your children unnecessary, but it is not even desirable. Children who grow up to be secure and confident get a *moderate* amount of attention from their parents. Not surprisingly, "helicopter parents" who pay too much attention to their kids are not really listening to what their children need any more than neglectful parents. In either extreme, chronic misattunement to the God-given need to connect causes shame. Psychologist Gershen Kaufman calls this the "breaking of the interpersonal bridge,"[5] which doesn't happen as a result of just a few instances of a parent failing to pay attention to a child's interpersonal needs. And the actual feeling of shame in and of itself is not always a bad thing. The momentary feeling of shame can be a feeling of smallness, like when you are standing beside an ocean or contemplating the universe and your tiny role in it. In fact, many theologians believe shame is the appropriate response when comparing yourself to God.[6] The feeling of shame reminds you that you are not God, and being mindful of that fact will save you a lot of grief in life.

GREG'S STORY

I have had the privilege of spending several weekends in the Louisiana State Penitentiary in Angola, Louisiana. I know that sounds strange, but I refer to my experiences there as a *privilege* because of the amazing work that Warden Burl Cain did in the twenty years he served as the warden there. He took what was once the bloodiest prison in America and transformed it into the safest institution for rehabilitation and moral change in the country. The prison, which is referred to simply as Angola by the locals, is the largest maximum security prison in the country, and 90 percent of the men sent there will never leave because they have been sentenced to life imprisonment for their crimes of murder, rape, and armed robbery.

One of the men I met there was Greg. Greg will die in Angola as punishment for the multiple people he murdered before arriving there. But in the several conversations I had with Greg, and most of them were with just the two of us alone in a room together, I never felt afraid or unsafe, not even for a moment. The Greg I met was a changed man. I am fully aware that Greg was once trapped in a life of shameful disregard for others, but that man no longer exists. Greg came face-to-face with his own shame, and he was never the same again.

Greg grew up in what he described as a performance-based household. If he struggled with anything, his parents didn't want to hear about it. He learned that if he did anything that was disruptive to their lives, he needed to keep it a secret. This led to a life of secrecy that caused him to split himself into two people—one whom he allowed his parents to see and another one who operated completely in the dark. Sadly, as the years passed, the things Greg did in the dark night of secrecy got worse and worse. He didn't feel good about most of the things he was doing behind his parents' backs, but because he could not bring his misdeeds into the light of day, they could never be addressed. Things eventually became so bad that Greg left home and ran away with some other guys doing pretty bad things that resulted in a life of crime, violence, and even murder. To symbolize the life he was living, and the prince of darkness he was following, Greg had the number 666 tattooed on his chest. That's how bad his situation was.

When Greg first came to Angola, he was still doing pretty bad things to other people, but now a feeling of futility was closing in on him. He was given a life sentence to prison for murder, and he had nowhere to run. He couldn't hide his shame in the dark anymore because now he had been exposed to the world as not just a man who had done bad things but as a man who was evil through and through. Greg believed the only reason the justice system sentences a man to life imprisonment is because he is so bad he can't be changed. Greg's imprisonment at Angola confirmed that his life was worthless to society, and this meant there was only one feeling left for him to feel about himself—shame.

Greg couldn't live with this feeling of shame being forced in his face daily for the rest of his life. He knew he would never leave Angola alive, so he made a plan to exit the prison on his own terms. The crushing feeling of insignificance that came with Greg's shame led him to devise a plan that would force others to never forget his name. His fantasy was that if he couldn't do anything to change this mind-numbing feeling of inferiority, he would leave this planet in an unforgettable way. At least then he would *be something*. Isn't that what it means if everyone remembers your name?

Greg's plan to reverse his insignificance was to fashion an ax out of the sheet metal that was available in the metal shop. He knew how to get into the shop, and he knew what he was going to do when he got there. Once he had his crudely formed ax, he was going to "make a mess of things" all the way to the front gate if he could get that far. He knew he would be shot and killed, but at least he would have done so much damage before they got to him that he would be remembered forever as the man who killed more people in Angola than anyone had ever even thought to do before. He wouldn't be insignificant anymore, not after he had done that. And he would never have to hide in secret again; everyone would know his name. At least that was his plan.

God, however, had a different plan for Greg. With his own ideas about how to deal with his shame in mind, Greg was making plans to get into the sheet metal shop. But just before this could happen, he found himself heading toward the prison chapel in the middle of the prison yard. He had never been in the chapel before, and he didn't care for the Christians that "hid out" there. The way he put it to me was, "To this day, I cannot tell you how I wound up with a signed clearance pass in my hand and standing in front of the chapel. So I just went in and sat down."[7] Greg found Chaplain McGee sitting there, miraculously, on his day off. In the next twenty minutes, Chaplain McGee introduced Greg to a loving God whom Greg didn't even know existed. Greg was at a life-or-death turning point. Was he going to *end* his life along with several others to escape the shame of insignificance, or *give* his life to a loving God who could heal it? Fortunately, he chose the latter, and he has never been the same since.

I am going to say a lot more about how God's grace heals shame later on, and I could say a bit about the psychological problems that Greg wrestles with too. My point here is that the shame Greg felt when he was authentically introduced to God gave him the opportunity to respond to a God that was greater than him, so much greater that he could make Greg feel accepted just as he was, faults, crimes, and all. Many people shrink back from this painful feeling of smallness when they are introduced to God, but Greg didn't that day. He knew something was very wrong in his life, but he had the courage to ask God to love him even when he couldn't love himself. Rather than hiding his shame, as he had done his entire life, Greg decided to expose it to God and ask for help. The rest is history. Greg is a changed man, and I can say this because I personally met him. He no longer worries about how to hide in the dark, because he is trying to live in the light of day all the time now. Ironically, even though shame was a major reason Greg ended up in a life of secrecy and crime, shame was instrumental in helping Greg turn to the God of the universe for help. When you see it from that perspective, shame is not always a bad thing. In fact, it appears that God has created it to play a very important role.

THE PROBLEM WITH SHAME

What causes shame to be a problem? The answer to this question requires just a bit of technical discussion. By age two we develop explicit memory, or the ability to remember things that are stored in the more rational left hemisphere of the brain. Now we can feel *and* symbolize things, and start to put them into words. With this capacity comes a more developed sense of self and a clearer capacity for recognizing the importance of our relationships with others. We now are not only seeking relationships, but we are making meaning out of our experiences. The way we make meaning is to organize our experiences based on how they feel. Feelings not only help us regulate our bodily experiences, but they also organize our relationships with others into experiences that are meaningful. Think about it. If something significant happens to you today, you will probably not cognitively remember the exact details of what happened a year from now. But you are not likely to forget how you felt. Feelings are organizers of experience. They are the vehicle by which we make meaning out of the important events in life.

Whenever you experience something significant, two things happen. First, you have a feeling. Then you make meaning out of the experience. The feeling comes first because the feeling part of the brain is faster than the thinking part. The feeling is the content of the experience, and the meaning you make out of it forms an unconscious belief.[8] These beliefs are unconscious because they are out of conscious awareness, not unconscious like being in a coma. They are automatic meanings we make out of emotional experiences, and we don't even know we are doing it.

For example, if you grow up with an abusive parent, your sense of safety will be damaged. As a child, you are dependent on your parent for your survival, so you have no choice but to feel vulnerable. But if the person you are dependent on is abusive, you learn quickly that every time you are vulnerable you get hurt. Then the feeling of vulnerability will automatically trigger the fear of abuse. So you develop the unconscious belief that vulnerability leads to abuse. The *meaning* that the feeling of vulnerability takes on for you is that it leads to mistreatment. From then on when you feel vulnerable, you automatically believe you are going to be exploited. The unconscious beliefs we form are involuntary meanings we make out of our emotional experiences. They help us organize our significant experiences, and they automatically organize every future experience from then on.

So why is this important? The problem with shame is not the feeling itself. As I mentioned, shame is a feeling of smallness, of being lesser or even inferior. The feeling itself can be transitory and fleeting. When it is, it can be helpful. For instance, if a huge guy with big muscles and a 666 tattoo on his chest rudely pushes past you on a street one night, you may instantly get an overwhelming feeling of inadequacy because you are irritated with the guy but immediately realize that you are no match for him. He is your superior physically, and your recognition of that fact is vital information. There is a hierarchy here, and you are the lesser or inferior person. This painful feeling of shame could quite possibly keep you out of the hospital and perhaps even save your life.

So the feeling of shame doesn't have to be a problem. But what it means to you unconsciously certainly can be. The problem with shame comes when you unconsciously organize it as defining your sense of self. Once shame triggers an unconscious belief that defines your sense of self as inferior, you don't just feel a momentary feeling of inferiority in comparison to someone else. You now come to believe that *who you are* is in fact inferior. Once shame becomes a principal organizer of your sense of self, you don't just recognize that you are not God, you can't help but feel that you are worthless at your very core. And it gets worse. Because unconscious beliefs are out of conscious awareness, they are experienced as a fact. Now you don't just believe you are worthless when you feel shame, you *know* you are worthless. What is just a *feeling* to some people is a *fact* to you. And what we all know is that beliefs can change, but facts can't. So when you are in the grips of the unconscious belief that all feelings of shame confirm your worthlessness as a human being, it is very hard to change this perception of yourself. Now shame is not just a painful feeling, it is a toxic confirmation of a moral defect in you that cannot be changed (at least, that is what it means to you). When this happens you are not just someone who feels shame, you are *shame-prone*.

SHAME-PRONENESS

One of the leading experts on the study of shame is Dr. June Price Tangney.[9] She has devoted her career to developing accurate measures of shame and distinguishing shame from guilt. After years of extensive research, she has concluded that shame is a very serious problem that leads to all kinds of interpersonal difficulties when people regularly respond to negative events with the feeling of shame. If you are predisposed to respond with shame, Dr. Tangney says you are *shame-prone*, and her research shows pretty convincingly that you are likely to suffer from several interpersonal and psychological problems.

You could say that the feeling of shame is a *state*, but when you become shame-prone, you can now be said to have the *trait* of shame. That's a problem. A shame-prone person repeatedly responds to negative events with the global feeling of being an inferior person, defective, worthless, and not belonging. A common response is to want to blame someone or something else, which then leads shame-prone people to get angry easily. And when they do get mad, their anger is often destructive because their capacity for empathy is compromised by the habitual feeling of shame. Even though the divine purpose of anger is energy to solve a problem,[10] shame-prone people aren't trying to fix anything when they get angry. They are just trying to blame someone else for their pain. And in the end, shame-prone people are motivated to hide. When we feel really bad about ourselves, we certainly don't want anyone to see us.

Dr. Tangney has conducted dozens of research studies linking shame-proneness to depression, chemical dependency, blame, PTSD, self-mutilation, suicide, panic attacks, severe anxiety problems, aggressiveness, procrastination, eating disorders, and the main cause of borderline and narcissistic personality disorders. Shame-proneness causes you to become self-focused, which is never good for your relationships, so it tends to drive away the very people you need to heal your damaged sense of self-worth. We now have a wealth of psychological research documenting that people who are predisposed to respond with shame suffer from personal psychological problems as well as interpersonal difficulties.

If shame-proneness is so damaging, why can't people just see this fact and change their feelings? As I said before, I hear from new patients all the time, "Just tell me what I need to do, and I'll change!" I would laugh if the problem wasn't so serious. The reason people can't just change shame-proneness is that they have moved from having states of shame to having the trait of shame. Or more specifically, people who are shame-prone are in the grips of very destructive unconscious beliefs. Any negative event that triggers the feeling of shame also triggers the unconscious belief that their *total sense of self* is worthless and unlovable. This is not a fleeting feeling of being lesser in the moment, but a crushing unconscious conviction that whatever just happened is a confirmation of a loathsome defect in themselves. And remember, when something is experienced in the unconscious—it is experienced as an unchangeable fact.

For many years Dr. Tangney conducted research project after research project finding the same conclusion: shame-proneness hurts people and their relationships. Her conclusions were so consistent that she believed there was no psychological benefit to shame at all. However, recently Dr. Tangney has started to come around to the idea that there might be some positive aspects to the *feeling* of shame.[11] She has started to find in her research what theologians have been saying for centuries—that feeling "lesser" is not always a bad thing. As the wisest man in history said, "The fear of the Lord is the beginning of knowledge, but fools despise wisdom and instruction" (Proverbs 1:7). Knowing your limitations and feeling inferior to God is the foundation of legitimate knowledge. Unbridled grandiosity is foolish, and it will eventually lead you to wrong conclusions in life. I think Dr. Tangney took a while to come to this realization because the real problem with shame is not the feeling itself but when we come to be convinced (unconsciously) that our very selves are permanently the source of shame. With most feelings, it is not the intensity of the feeling itself that causes us problems, but what the feeling comes to *mean* to us about our sense of self. *Feeling* inferior is not the same thing as believing you actually *are* inferior.

SELF-CONSCIOUS EMOTIONS

Guilt and shame are referred to as self-conscious emotions because they are feelings you have that refer to your sense of self. You may have noticed that I use the term *sense of self* instead of referring to you having *a self*. Although saying shame is a feeling you have about your "self" is simpler, saying shame is a feeling you have about your "sense of self" is more accurate. A common mistake people make is to refer to having a self like they have a brain or a liver or a heart. Just because you have a discrete physical body that contains bodily parts within it doesn't mean that you are a discrete psychological entity that contains independent parts like a self or a mind. The notion that you are a container of psychological parts is based on what psychologists and philosophers call the *Cartesian Error*.[12]

René Descartes put forth the idea "I think, therefore I am," which resulted in a widespread belief in Western culture that we each have an individual mind within our separate selves that can independently reason its own way to truth. Neuroscientists have now disproven this notion, and the current thinking in science is that both our emotions and our thoughts go into making up our "minds" about things, and all of that is dependent on the context of our relationships with others.

In other words, you don't have a separate self or a mind that is isolated from what other people think and feel. Instead, you are fundamentally a relational person. I don't have a self that can be identified with an X-ray machine or physical exam. Mark (that's me) has a sense of self. That forces me to realize that my very identity is dependent on the relationships I have with God and others. Believing that I am an individual self isolated from others is just an illusion to protect me from how frightening it is to be so radically dependent on them to know who I am.

Researchers of infants are telling us now that humans have a sense of self from the moment of birth, and that sense of self develops throughout the lifetime. Because guilt and shame are self-conscious emotions, they too are developing from birth on. This means that some people are predisposed to respond to negative events with the feeling of shame because of experiences they had that they will never specifically remember. It is possible to begin developing the feeling quite early that who you are is somehow defective and inferior, which means that your implicit memory of feeling worthless can be triggered and you won't even realize it is happening. Future negative events can stimulate unconscious beliefs that reinforce your negative view of your sense of self. I'm saying that some shame-prone people are in the grips of unconscious processes that they have had their entire lives. So if you are starting to think that you might be one of those shame-prone people I'm talking about, at least you can know that it is not your fault that you got this way. The bad feelings you have been wrestling with may have started long before you can even remember.

As one psychologist puts it, shame starts as a two-person experience but then morphs into a one-person story.[13] Shame is the result of interpersonal experiences where we fail to connect and end up feeling worthless because of our failure. This emotional invalidation of our ontological need to relate to God and others has interpersonal roots but then takes on a life of its own when our sense of self becomes organized as shameful. Then we automatically respond with shame because we don't need anyone else to make us feel inadequate; we have come to believe that we are inadequate all on our own.

The Fall

The Bible tells us that God created Adam and Eve for the purpose of having intimate relationships with him, and that in the beginning "Adam and his wife were both naked, and they felt no shame" (Genesis 2:25). Their nakedness was pure vulnerability, with no fear. Because of the unconditional acceptance they felt in their relationships with God and their lack of self-consciousness, they did not experience being less than God as painful evidence that they were worthless beings. This was God's original intent for us, to live in joyful relationship with him. The Westminster Catechism puts it this way: "What is the chief end of man? Man's chief end is to glorify God, and to enjoy him forever."

Adam and Eve rejected their relationships with God when they decided they didn't just want to have relationships with God; they instead wanted to be just like him. The notable thing here is that Adam's story is our story. We all were created for joyful relationships with God and others, free from the shame-proneness that cripples our capacities for love and connection. But at some point the temptations of life bring insecurities that make us want something more. Fearing that who we are and what we have are not enough, we decide to be our own gods and take matters into our own hands. Refusing to accept ourselves as we are, we strive to create defenses against the self-conscious feeling of shame. Adam and Eve chose to eat of the forbidden tree because they were told "when you eat from it your eyes will be opened, and you will be like God" (Genesis 3:5).

Of course this passage is too theologically rich for us to deal with it completely, but you get the point. When we refuse to accept the sense of self that we were created for, a joyful relationship with God who is greater than us, we become painfully aware that we are inadequate to actually be God, and our sense of self starts to feel worthless in comparison. As counselor and speaker John Bradshaw puts it, shame is the core and the consequence of the Fall.[14] When being less than God becomes something painful that we want to escape, we become excruciatingly self-conscious and need to hide. "Then the eyes of both of them were opened, and they realized they were naked; so they sewed fig leaves together and made coverings for themselves" (Genesis 3:7).

If you think that you might be shame-prone, you are going to be tempted to blame your parents for your predisposition to respond with shame. While they certainly played a role in making you who you are, the Genesis story brings out one more point I want to make about shame. None of us had perfect parents, but none of our parents had perfect children either. Obviously, Adam and Eve *did* have a perfect Parent, and they still ended up mismanaging their shame. Some children are born into this world with greater sensitivity to light, a greater reactivity to heat and cold, higher anxiety, higher cortisol levels in the brain, and in short, a greater likelihood of experiencing the breaking of their interpersonal bridges. For those children, even if their parents were perfect they still might end up shame-prone. I don't think it is helpful to figure out who to blame for the shame we have in our lives (shame-prone people tend to blame others anyway), but I do think it is helpful to figure out what to do about it. That is the point of the story of the Fall. What Adam and Eve fell *from* was their relationships with God, and then consequently with each other. This is what we all are seeking to restore so we can live in joyful relationships with him and others forever.

At the end of your life, on your deathbed, you are not going to say, "Gee, I wish I had made more money," or "Gosh, I wish I had accomplished more things." No, if you have any regrets at all, you are going to say, "Gee, I wish I had been a better husband (or wife)," or "Gosh, I wish I had spent more time with the people I love." In the end only your relationships will matter. That is why you are here. Shame can help you or it can hurt you in your efforts to have better relationships. We are going to spend the next several chapters together understanding exactly how.

CHAPTER THREE

The Power of Vulnerability

In June of 2010, a little-known researcher from the University of Houston recorded a TED Talk titled "The Power of Vulnerability" to try to explain her scientific findings in everyday language in hopes that people outside of the ivory towers of academia might find some benefit in her work. Scientists often wonder if anyone is listening to them. As of today that TED Talk has been viewed more than 30 million times, making it one of the most viewed TED Talks ever, and that researcher has gone on to publish three number one *New York Times* bestsellers. Her name is Brené Brown and she has dedicated her career to studying the importance of vulnerability for psychological health, and millions of people have been helped by what she has taught them. Much to her surprise, people were listening.

Brown is very honest about her own struggles with vulnerability and how she had to go to therapy before she was able to practice what she learned from her own research. The people she found to be living the richest lives with the most satisfying relationships she called "wholehearted." These were the people who had the courage to face difficulties, the self-esteem to accomplish their goals, and the joy to live life to its fullest. Although living vulnerably is the opposite of being in control of all the variables (which is what researchers are trained to do), Brown is now convinced that vulnerability is the key to living life in the best and most meaningful way possible. And specifically when it comes to the issue of shame, Brown believes that vulnerability has the power to make you feel that you are *enough*, the exact opposite of what shame makes you feel.

Of course, the path to the best things in life is never easy. Brown also found in her research that we all fight the very thing we need to help us live better lives. While almost all of us admire vulnerability when we see it in others, none of us want to practice it ourselves.[1] We absolutely love to see the raw truth displayed by others but are afraid to let them see it in us. In short, we both love vulnerability and fear it. It is only when we are most vulnerable that we can experience the connection with God and others that we were designed for, but it is also exactly when we are most vulnerable that we can get hurt the most. Vulnerability is a two-edged sword that can cut both ways. It can surgically heal you of your deepest shame or cut out your heart. That's just how it is with vulnerability.

I know Jesus was talking about the cost of discipleship when he said, "Whoever wants to save their life will lose it, but whoever loses their life for me will find it" (Matthew 16:25), but he was also making a psychologically profound statement about vulnerability at the same time. What Jesus was saying about your spiritual life, Brown has discovered is just as true about your psychological life. The harder you try to defend yourself and hold on to who you think you are, the harder it is to find the true meaning of life. Only through surrendering your defensive view of yourself can you find genuine connection to God and others, and that is the only place the true meaning of your life can be found.

WHAT IS VULNERABILITY?

To start with, vulnerability is not just being open. I'm sure you know people who take great pride in how open they are. They will say things like, "You can ask me anything," or "My life is an open book," as if they are the truly courageous people and the rest of us are just too timid to "spill the beans" on ourselves like they do. But if you think about it, you probably feel somewhat awkward when people say things like this. It doesn't really draw you to them, and it doesn't actually make you want to take your clothes off and jump in the truth or dare pool with them either.

These are people who are open about the facts of their lives (and the lives of others) but don't really make themselves vulnerable. They are more than willing to give you information about themselves but not in a way that exposes them to the possibility of getting hurt. But the *real* truth is, it's not really being vulnerable if you can't get hurt in the process. Openness used in this way can actually be a form of calling attention to yourself. It's not about connecting with other people; it's more about getting attention.

Vulnerability is taking the risk to expose yourself emotionally. You will feel very uncertain while doing it, but there is no other path to the most meaningful experiences you will ever have. We were created for the purpose of connection to God and others, and vulnerability is the requirement for achieving that purpose. Vulnerability is the state in which we all come into the world. From the very first moments of your life, you were vulnerable, and how well you were able to connect to others around you while you were that vulnerable determined how you felt about yourself then, and it continues to define your sense of self today.

Donald Winnicott, the most often quoted psychoanalytic pediatrician, is famous for having said, "There is no such thing as a baby."[2] What he meant was, you can't talk about an infant without talking about that infant's relationship to the person caring for him or her. Our very identity is dependent on our relationships with those who care for us. Because we are fundamentally relational beings, we are fundamentally vulnerable. Psychologists no longer talk about humans having an individual self, we talk about having a sense of self in the context of our relationships. For you to be you, you need God and others.

HAVING NEEDS DOESN'T MAKE YOU NEEDY

A common myth that I battle with my clients is the notion that vulnerability is a weakness. It's true that you can get hurt by being vulnerable—that's the very definition of vulnerability. But getting hurt doesn't mean you are weak. Getting hurt emotionally isn't the same thing as getting hurt physically. Physical hurt can indicate that you are in a weakened condition with compromised physical strength. But getting hurt emotionally can indicate the exact opposite. It is actually through our painful emotional experiences that we learn life's greatest lessons. Our greatest insights, most intimate connections with others, and the development of our most crucial capacities to deal with life come in the emotional valleys, not during our mountaintop experiences.

Avoiding physical pain is a good thing; avoiding emotional pain is not. Jesus said, "Whoever does not take up their cross and follow me is not worthy of me" (Matthew 10:38). And he wasn't kidding. This wasn't just a metaphor for Jesus, because he ended up dragging *his* cross to his own crucifixion. Jesus taught a lot about joy and love, but he never taught his followers to avoid pain. Quite the opposite, it was central to Jesus's teachings that facing suffering well is a crucial element in developing a mature character and that our vulnerability to suffering is not only not a bad thing but is the best path to finding a clear picture of who God really is. To Jesus vulnerability was certainly not a weakness but was actually a sign of spiritual strength.

Related to the myth that vulnerability is a weakness is the equally wrongheaded notion that having needs makes you needy. Pop psychology went through several stages of reinforcing this myth a few years ago, and some people still hang on to this outdated concept. People would say, "I can't make *you* feel anything. If you are angry because of what I said, well then, that's your problem." This type of thinking is based on the theory that all that matters is getting your feelings out. The more you express yourself, the more authentic you are. Getting all those stored-up feelings out was only a good thing. If other people got hurt, you could just say to them, "You can't handle the truth!"

We now know this is just bad psychology. To be the best version of you, you need other people. If you hurt other people, you *should* feel bad about that. You have a moral and psychological responsibility to others, and you need an emotional connection to them to be psychologically healthy. Now, I am not saying that every time someone gets her or his feelings hurt that it is your fault, but I am saying that it is in your best interest to care about it. I can make you feel things and you can make me feel things too. We are not just two ships passing in the night.[3] We are made by God for the purpose of relationship with him and others, and psychologists now know we are hardwired from birth to be seeking out relationships. Having emotional needs doesn't make you needy, it makes you human. And quite the opposite from trying to pretend that you don't have needs, you should be trying to uncover exactly what they are so you can find a way to share them with others in ways that connect you to them. Needs are not something to be ashamed of; both your needs and the needs of those you love are the substance of your most important relationships.

SO, WHAT ARE YOU AFRAID OF?

When we talk about being vulnerable, we have to ask, "Vulnerable to what?" I am not talking about vulnerability to being physically hurt, militarily blindsided, or financially devastated. When I talk about vulnerability, I am talking about being vulnerable to feelings. Feelings are what create connection, and feelings are what we fear when we are vulnerable. So the next time a situation arises when you are called on to be vulnerable, you will have to answer the question "What are you afraid of?" The answer is: feelings. That's what will happen to you when you make yourself vulnerable. You are going to feel something uncomfortable, and learning to deal with that discomfort will make you a better person.

For instance, fear is the uncomfortable feeling that signals impending danger. This is a good thing. A fearless person is a foolish person. Fear triggers our natural fight, flight, or freeze response. In the face of danger, you will first take a moment to assess the situation, and then either retreat or attack depending on your assessment. Having fear is usually not a problem, but what it means to you for having it can be a problem.

The people whom we typically think of as fearful people are almost always dealing with another problem that lies hidden out of sight. In almost every case, fearful people are dealing with shame. People who get stuck in the freeze, fight, or flight response are trapped there because they see their fear as evidence of a shameful weakness in themselves. They don't see their fear as crucial information alerting them to some danger they need to deal with; they automatically believe their fear is a confirmation of a weakness buried deep within them that is now being exposed to everyone around.

Shame is not only a self-conscious emotion, but it causes people to be self-focused as well. Shame is a painful feeling that directs your attention onto yourself in ways that make it difficult for you to care about what other people are feeling around you. Your own feelings of defectiveness become so weighty for you that your attention is diverted into coming up with strategies to hide. Shame-proneness causes people to mismanage their fear over and over again. Rather than using fear as a signal that directs your attention outward toward some approaching problem, shame forces you to direct your attention inward toward a bigger problem you don't want to face—painful feelings of inadequacy. Shame-prone people tend to respond to fear by either trying to hide or trying forcefully to overcome it. But the best response to fear is neither of these strategies. The best response to fear is to face it, with vulnerability.

Too Afraid to Be Vulnerable

Drew and Nicole came to marriage counseling a little late. What I mean by this is that people often wait for years before they come for help, struggling with the same pattern of fighting over and over again with nothing changing. It's really too bad, because in the vast majority of cases, marriage counseling helps. And Drew and Nicole certainly needed it.

Drew is a successful businessman and Nicole is an accomplished architect. They have two wonderful kids and a beautiful home, and they are involved in their local church. But even though their lives looked good to everyone on the outside, what went on within the walls of their spacious house wasn't so good.

Nicole is an attractive and energetic woman who is both a very involved mother and a successful architect, which means she has two full-time jobs and is good at both of them. She is passionate and excited about life, traits to which Drew was immediately attracted when he met her. Drew is more of an introvert than Nicole, and his serious attitude about his career and finances gave Nicole a peaceful feeling of security when she met him. *This guy would be a good father*, she thought, and his non-confrontational manner made her feel safe.

But as happens with most marriages, what attracts us to our partners at first eventually becomes a source of irritation later. Nicole grew up with an alcoholic mother who would yell at her for the smallest things, and if she had been drinking too much would even hit her in a rage. This unstable environment wreaks havoc on a child's sense of self, so the unpredictable and abusive atmosphere of her childhood left Nicole with a shame-proneness that she tried to keep hidden as best she could. Consequently, what started out in their marriage as a passionate and frequently excited Nicole, morphed into a critical and angry Nicole as the years went on.

Drew, on the other hand, was always an even-tempered and thoughtful person. At first this is exactly what Nicole wanted—the opposite of her mother. But as the years went on, what was originally a securely non-confrontational Drew morphed into a withdrawn and depressed Drew in response to his conflict with Nicole.

The pattern that Drew and Nicole developed in their marriage is a common one. Each time conflict would arise and one of them got hurt feelings, they both had their own *deeply engrained* responses. Drew would withdraw and Nicole would attack. Each response was equally powerful in hurting the other, and both were convinced that the other person was the root of their marital problems. Nicole was convinced that Drew's depression and emotional withdrawal were damaging their marriage and their children, and Drew was convinced that Nicole's rages were doing irreparable damage to everyone she unleashed them on, especially him.

The problem in their marriage was that neither Nicole nor Drew understood the problem in their marriage. When they finally came in for help, all they knew was that they both were very angry. Drew was mad at Nicole for her unbridled displays of rage directed at him, and Nicole was just as mad at Drew for the way he had emotionally cut her off. That, she insisted, was the reason she was so infuriated with him. What neither could see was that the very thing they were doing to deal with the conflict in the marriage was causing the other person to respond the way they were. Nicole's angry attacks would make Drew withdraw, and Drew's withdrawal would make Nicole angrily pursue him. This withdrawal-pursuit cycle had been going round and round for years with no one able to get off the merry-go-round of dysfunction.

What I was eventually able to get Nicole and Drew to realize was that they were both afraid. Anger is a secondary emotion, which means that there is always another emotion underneath it that is more primary. In their case, both Nicole and Drew were not just angry, they were both afraid. Nicole was afraid she would live the rest of her adult life as lonely and unloved as she had been in her childhood, and Drew was afraid that who he was simply was not enough for her and that her disgust of him was proof that he was incapable of earning her respect. Nicole's anger made him feel worthless, and Drew's withdrawal made her feel exactly the same way. Although neither of them said it out loud before they came to therapy, both were afraid they had lost their value to the other. And that feeling of worthlessness was killing them both inside.

After many sessions of active refereeing on my part—and I do mean *active*, for I don't allow couples to hurt each other in the marital counseling I do—I was able to get Drew and Nicole to understand their problem. The reason they were fighting was that they each felt disconnected from the other, and living disconnected in a marriage violates the very purpose for which humans were made. Drew wasn't withdrawing because he no longer loved Nicole; he was just trying not to make things worse. He wasn't going to yell and scream like she did, so he thought keeping quiet was the best choice. Nicole wasn't raging at Drew because she didn't respect him; she was trying to get through to the only man she has ever loved, and she didn't know how to get him to listen to how much she needed him to make her feel safe again. She wasn't going to keep silent about the disconnection in their marriage; this was too important to not get upset about it.

Once they understood they were fighting for connection, things could change for Nicole and Drew. Nicole could soften her approach, and Drew could open up about how he felt about things. As it turned out, the problem was not that Nicole was too angry or that Drew was too emotionally unavailable, but that both of them were *too afraid to be vulnerable*. So mistakenly, they each tried to deal with that fear in exactly the wrong way. Nicole tried to overcome her fear by demanding that Drew pay attention to her, and Drew tried to deny his fear and pretend that nothing could hurt him behind his wall of silence. Both strategies were based on avoiding vulnerability at all costs. But what they learned was that the only way to truly deal with fear is to face it—*with* vulnerability.

As Drew came out from behind his stone wall of invulnerability, Nicole could drop her wall of rage, which she was hiding behind as well. And as Nicole could vulnerably admit her fears of never being lovable, which were the real reason for her rage, Drew could easily confess how much he loved and needed her in his life. As Nicole softened, Drew engaged emotionally; and as Drew engaged, Nicole couldn't help but melt into him.

Although it is difficult to do, the best cure for the *fear* of vulnerability is to have the courage to be vulnerable. When vulnerability is done in the right way, it has the power to change us and everyone around us. Seriously mismanaged cases of the fight, flight, and freeze response like Nicole's and Drew's require professional help.

They were so stuck in their anger-withdrawal cycle that they couldn't get out of it by themselves. You, too, may need help risking vulnerability as the most effective way to face your fears, but the power of vulnerability to get you unstuck in life is there for you when you are ready.

THE FEAR OF DEPENDENCY

If you have a fear of vulnerability, you almost certainly also have a fear of dependency. The reason we fear vulnerability is because we can get hurt by depending on other people. If you don't depend on anyone other than yourself, well then, no one will ever disappoint you. And if you don't depend on anyone, you never have a need to be vulnerable. Convincing yourself that dependency is a bad thing fixes both problems at the same time. At least that is what some people want to believe.

Fear of dependency can take you in one of two directions: individualism or a victim mentality. *Individualism* is the belief that you can be sufficient all by yourself. Personal power is power over other people, and looking out for number one is the most essential thing you can do. Individualism makes the Cartesian Error I mentioned earlier by believing that I can make up my own mind, be objective, and reason my way to truth without the influence of anyone else. But people who are rigidly individualistic are not that way because they are self-confident; rather, they fear dependency.

Self-centeredness is not self-confidence. Minimizing my need for other people is not a strength; it is a fear of surrendering control. Neuroscientists tell us that the human sense of self is *dependent* on emotional responses from other people for the brain to develop properly.[4] For you to be you, you are dependent on emotional connections with others. That dependency makes you vulnerable to getting hurt, but it doesn't change the fact that you were created to be dependent on God and others. That is just the way you were made.

Psychoanalyst Robert Stolorow calls this idea that we don't need others "the myth of the isolated mind."[5] He calls it a myth because humans don't have a mind like they have a brain. What we refer to as "mind" is actually the result of all our relational interactions. We can think thoughts because we have brains, but we only *know* we think thoughts because our sense of having a "mind" was developed from bouncing off of all the relational encounters we have had over the course of our lifetimes. We are always looking through a lens that was shaped by our history of relationships, and this is what gives each of us the sense of being different from other people.

Now that we understand the human sense of self as radically dependent on our relationships, many of the statements Jesus made about his dependency on God, and our dependency on him, make more sense to us. He said, "Believe me when I say that I am in the Father and the Father is in me" (John 14:11). While he was making a statement about his divinity that he uniquely shared with God, he was also making a psychologically accurate statement about the dependency of his sense of self on his relationship with God, which is something that we all have in common. In referring to his relationships with us, Jesus went on to say, "I am the vine; you are the branches. If you remain in me and I in you, you will bear much fruit; apart from me you can do nothing" (John 15:5). He had a firm grasp of the fact that true identity is rooted in relationships with him and with God, and that the pursuit of individual identity could only produce something false, or a myth, at best. Jesus understood how our sense of self is developed thousands of years before neuroscience could be invented to prove that it is true.

The second direction a fear of dependency will take you is toward a *victim mentality*.[6] Anyone can be victimized by violence or abuse, and learning that being a victim of abuse was not your fault is a key part of your recovery. But being a victim is not the same thing as *believing* that you are a victim. People who believe they are victims have a victim mentality based on the conviction that they are powerless. They actually fear that their dependency on others proves that they are powerless to run their own lives, and they live with a deep-seated conviction that vulnerability is a weakness. To them dependency is not a sign of strength but shameful evidence that they are weak. To them having needs means they are needy, and for that they are very, very ashamed.

Tragically, those with a victim mentality look for others to agree with them. Well-meaning people come in and out of their lives trying to help them, but they don't actually want help to change; they want help to confirm their powerlessness. Eventually they find someone who also believes that victims are powerless, and they enter into what I call the *victim trap* of endless energy being poured into a black hole that doesn't change anything. Everyone in the victim trap believes that dominance is power and that a dependent person is a weak person. Why would anyone ever adopt a victim mentality? Well, of course, because that person is shame-prone. A person has to be thoroughly convinced of their own worthlessness to make the victim trap work.

HEALTHY DEPENDENCE

The fear of vulnerability leads to a prohibition against hope. That is, after you have tried to be vulnerable and gotten hurt too many times in the past, to protect yourself from future disappointments, you refuse to allow yourself to hope. This can look like depression, but it is actually something different. People who refuse to hope also

refuse to allow joy to enter into their lives. They can be happy from
time to time, but they don't experience lasting joy. And since we
were created for joyful relationship with God and others, this causes
them to feel that something is very, very wrong. And what do they
conclude is wrong? They are.

People who have a prohibition against hope are unable to be vulnerable in ways that can heal them of any painful feelings of shame.
When this inability to be vulnerable continues for any length of
time, the result is that they become shame-prone. This fear of vulnerability and refusal to allow for any feelings of hope can entrench
people in a pattern of self-conscious isolation for years. This, of
course, is not how we were created to live.

The solution to the fear of vulnerability is healthy dependence.
Psychologists call it *secure attachment*. People who live with secure
attachments view vulnerability as a powerful means for connection, and they experience their dependence on others as a natural
part of the give-and-take of healthy interdependence. People with
secure attachments strive for joyful relationships over happy experiences and understand that they can have joy even in the midst
of extremely difficult circumstances. The apostle Paul called it the
"peace of God, which transcends all understanding" (Philippians
4:7). We feel this joy because of our connections to God and others, independent of whatever suffering we might be going through.
It is not something we can *understand*; it is only something we can
experience.

In addition, psychologists have discovered that people who have
secure attachments are generally grateful people. Practicing gratitude is the way you work through your prohibition against hope.
This doesn't mean you live in denial of the difficulty of your circumstances; that would be a false optimism that is very irritating to the
people around you. No, true gratitude is to look for something good

in the midst of your troubles. Don't deny that your problems exist; try to find something for which you can be grateful. It may be something as simple as the sun on your face or the clean air after a rain, but practicing gratitude opens the door for joy to return into your relationships, and you need that for dealing with any fear of vulnerability you might have.

People with secure attachments are not looking for the easy way out. The way Brené Brown puts it is, "we don't get comfortable with hard conversations; we normalize discomfort."[7] I like that. If you are comfortable, you probably aren't learning anything. Growth stretches us, and that means we need to believe that discomfort is simply a normal part of life. People with secure attachments aren't afraid of that because they have the connections they need to support them through the discomfort. The best life isn't about getting onto easy street, it's about being connected to God and others no matter where you live. The goal isn't to be better than everyone else by invulnerably rising above them; it's to figure out how to have a healthy dependence on God and others to find joy.

CHAPTER FOUR

Humility Has Nothing
to Do with Humiliation

Some people think there are two kinds of shame: a healthy shame and an unhealthy one. One will help you do good things and the other won't. I don't think this is quite right. It's not really that there are two kinds of shame; there is just the feeling of shame, and then whether or not it triggers the belief that you are *permanently* worthless every time you feel it. There is a difference between "I *feel* worthless" and "I *am* worthless." The problem occurs when you experience the feeling of shame unconsciously as evidence that you are worthless (this is the unconscious belief I was talking about in chapter 2). This takes place when you already have the unconscious belief that you are worthless, and then when you feel the feeling of shame it confirms this belief. Now you have the feeling of shame and the gut-wrenching conviction that you are a worthless human being on top of it. So shame-prone people are struggling with their sense of self-worth before they ever do anything that makes them feel shame. They seem to be constantly looking for reasons to feel shame. And what do you think happens when you are looking for reasons to feel something? You find it.

On the other hand, you could be a person with relatively high self-esteem who is not carrying around a lot of doubts about your self-worth. Negative things happen, and you might even feel shame because of them, but you don't often experience the automatic triggering of beliefs of permanent worthlessness. To you, feeling shame doesn't mean anything in particular about your self-worth because you started off with a relatively good sense of worthiness. For you to have feelings of shame *sometimes* is normal, but you are able to go in and out of feelings of shame easily and you don't get stuck there. You feel shame, but you are not shame-prone.

You should have times when you feel inferior or less than others. As I mentioned earlier, having this feeling when you vulnerably approach God is a good thing. Some of the greatest saints throughout history reported that the more time they spent in God's presence, the more they were aware of their shame. For instance, Isaiah's first response to seeing God at his commission was "Woe to me…!" (Isaiah 6:5), and Moses's response to hearing God call him to free his people was "Who am I…?" (Exodus 3:11). But vulnerably being in God's presence will confirm for you both your realization that you are far less than God *and* that you are also very valuable at the same time. It is possible to feel inferior and that you have worth simultaneously. This is not a different kind of shame; it is the ability to feel shame and to believe that you are precious in God's eyes at the same time. One doesn't have to cancel out the other.

This is also the explanation for the two kinds of guilt I mentioned in chapter 1. Guilt based on love stimulates you to repair any damage you have done to relationships, while neurotic guilt based on shame stimulates you to hide from getting caught. The explanation for the unhealthiness of neurotic guilt is that you are also feeling shame at the same time you are feeling guilt. The reason people with neurotic guilt only feel bad because they got caught (rather than feeling bad for having done what they did) is that they have feelings of shame that make them feel defective, worthless, and inferior. Their shame-proneness causes them to want to hide, which makes making amends for their wrongdoing very difficult. The neurotic guilt of people who feel bad most of the time and punish themselves with continuous emotional self-flagellation is rooted in feelings of shame that never get addressed. So it is more accurate to say that the real problem for people with neurotic guilt is that they are shame-prone and are not dealing with their shame.

While there aren't actually two kinds of shame, there is a distinction between people who feel shame and people who are shame-prone. Shame-prone people regularly feel bad about themselves when negative things happen, and this grinds down their self-worth over time. Like developing the bad habit of slapping yourself every time you make a mistake, feeling bad about yourself every time something negative happens is eventually going to leave a mark.

HUMILITY IS NOT HUMILIATION

Another distinction that is important to make is the difference between humility and humiliation. Although this is a difficult thing for us to grasp in Western cultures, humility is actually a positive feature of psychological health. We don't consider it a virtue, but it is. Most Westerners lump humility in with vulnerability and consider it a weakness. We confuse it with humiliation, which is not a good thing. Almost everyone would say they should be ashamed of themselves at times, but no one believes they ever deserve to be humiliated.

Humiliation is public shame and prolonged embarrassment. People are humiliated when they feel exposed to ridicule and powerless to hide from it. The core response to shame is the desire to hide, and humiliation is the crushing feeling of public shame when you have no opportunity for escape. It is like the scene in the movie *The Elephant Man* when John Merrick's cloak of disguise over his seriously deformed body is ripped from him by a crowd of curiously horrified onlookers. He crumples in a heap, nakedly exposed with nowhere to hide, only able to cry, "I am not an animal! I am not an animal! I am a human being," as his solitary pathetic response. With the physical evidence of his undeniable defectiveness exposed to all, he felt condemned to a life of inescapable rejection by humanity. That is the picture of humiliation.

Humiliation is everyone's worst nightmare. Each of us was created for loving connection, but humiliation is the searing shame of having our deepest, darkest evidence of worthlessness exposed to others in a way that leaves us isolated and alone. Make no mistake about it, if you ever thought that someone deserved to be humiliated in hopes that it would teach him or her a lesson, you were wrong. Humiliation is never a good thing.

Humility has nothing to do with humiliation. As Jesus was finishing his last supper with his disciples, he was struck with the thought "that the Father had put all things under his power, and that he had come from God and was returning to God" (John 13:3). This was hardly a moment of insecurity on his part. In fact, it was obviously quite the opposite. With more confidence in his worth and value than any other human being had ever had, Jesus chose exactly that moment to wrap a towel around his waist and wash the feet of his friends. In an amazing act of humility (which the disciples couldn't understand), he simply said, "Now that I, your Lord and Teacher, have washed your feet, you also should wash one another's feet. I have set you an example that you should do as I have done for you" (John 13:14-15).

Incredible. This was Jesus's teaching on power. The most

powerful way to lead others is with humility. He was turning every-thing they knew about power on its head. To have the most pow-erful effect on others, you first need to know who you are and then serve them with love. Humility has nothing to do with feeling defec-tive and worthless, and it is the opposite of exposing your weakness to others, which disconnects you from them. Humility is having the confidence to serve others because you know you have something of value to offer them. Humility is considering the needs of others with respect and having the courage to be vulnerable to them by your willingness to serve them. Humility is not a form of weakness; it is a manifestation of power. In Western cultures, however, we have a hard time grasping this concept.

Susan's Story

Susan grew up as the only daughter of a working-class couple in a small town in England where people worked hard, took responsibil-ity for themselves, and did their best to be good neighbors. It never occurred to anyone to go to therapy; there weren't any psycholo-gists around anyway. If anyone did have a problem, they would go to see the Catholic priest. That is what people had been doing there for hundreds of years, and if that was good enough for their ances-tors, it was good enough for them today.

Like most kids in her community, Susan attended the local Catholic school associated with her parish. The education there was good, and the nuns were strict. But unlike most kids in her commu-nity, Susan didn't just follow the rules because she was told to do so. Perhaps it was her God-given personality, or maybe it was the con-fidence she developed as a result of the unshakable belief that her father had in her, but Susan found it impossible to keep quiet if she disagreed with something, no matter who was speaking. Well, in those days this was just not something that the nuns of her school saw as a strength. Quite the opposite, they saw it as a defiant quality of a sinful nature that needed to be punished. And what was their preferred technique for punishing sin? Humiliation.

"Susan, I want you to stand and give me a four-minute recitation on the reconciliation of the concept of purgatory with the concept of an all-powerful and loving God," Sister Mary Ellen announced. "I will give you two minutes to prepare."

In just over sixty seconds, Susan stood erect by her chair and launched into her perfectly logical soliloquy: "If God is all-loving and all-powerful, and if purgatory is a torturous place where defenseless people are subjected to cruel punishment, then it follows that God cannot be the creator of purgatory, as it is *ipso facto* illogical to reconcile these two concepts with each other."

Then Susan promptly sat down. And just as her crisply ironed skirt hit her chair, Sister Mary Ellen shrieked, "Susan! You wicked child. You will leave this classroom immediately and report to the headmaster's chambers, where you will recite sixty Hail Marys. And if you only do fifty-nine, God will know!"

And so it would go with Susan until she was finally able to graduate from the local parish high school and go on to university. And Susan *did* go on. Having been fascinated by the power of the relational bonds she witnessed her father have in her community, and completely disillusioned by the rigid and shaming approach to relationships of the church, Susan rejected her association to the Catholic Church and turned to the study of psychology for the answers to the deeper questions in life. *What is love?* she wondered. *What makes a marriage work?* she asked herself after her parents' separation. *What does it mean to live well?* Susan wanted to know.

Susan left England and came to North America in search of her answers. She went on to earn her doctorate and become a distinguished professor of clinical psychology and the bestselling author of books on marriage and healthy relationships. Today Dr. Susan Johnson is one of the leading authorities on marital therapy in the world, and literally millions of people are living better and more loving lives because of her research and teaching.

But Susan's story doesn't end here. Because of her God-given abilities and the strength of her father's love that protected her from turning to shame-proneness as a result of the nuns' treatment of her, Susan went on to develop Emotionally Focused Marital Therapy (EFT),[1] one of the most powerful techniques for helping marriages that has ever been conceived. Thousands of therapists all over the world have studied this technique, and it has become the most empirically documented approach to helping marriages that we have today. Because of the effectiveness of her approach, all kinds of therapists have sought out this training, including Kenneth Sanderfer, a Christian therapist from Tennessee. Kenneth was a former missionary and committed to the ministry of helping marriages, especially within the Christian church. He could see the parallels between EFT and Jesus's teachings, in spite of the fact that Susan had no desire to have this conversation with him whatsoever.

EFT teaches that human beings are fundamentally dependent on relationships for their security and sense of self. Jesus taught that we are created in the relational image of God, dependent on him for our very being. EFT teaches that the goal of life is to repair broken relationships. Jesus said that he had come to restore relationships to God. EFT teaches that you cannot live well without a secure attachment. Jesus taught us that God is the ultimate source of secure attachment.

For years Kenneth tried to get Susan to consider what the Bible had to say about relationships, and how what she was doing was actually completely compatible with a Christian worldview. But this was not Susan's experience of Christianity. The shaming treatment she received at the hands of her childhood teachers was certainly not compatible with her mission of creating connections. She knew that. But there always had been one nagging exception that Susan just couldn't ignore—Father Anthony Storey.

Father Anthony was a priest who befriended Susan when she was an undergraduate student back in England. He was a remarkably Christlike figure on campus who was well known to be the person you could go to in times of need. It didn't matter what hour of the day, who you were, or what the nature of your problem was, Father Anthony was there for you. Buddhist students, Muslim students, Jewish students, Catholics and Protestants alike all went to Father Anthony for help. And when Susan needed help, he was right there for her as well.

Even though Susan had rejected the Catholic Church, Father Anthony never rejected her. Throughout her life, during times of need, Susan would turn to Father Anthony for his wise counsel and support. He didn't demand that she have the correct theology, and he didn't care if her philosophy of life was illogical or not, he just loved Susan and gave her a secure attachment to come home to whenever she needed it. And years later when Susan wrote to him about her revolutionary scientific discoveries about love and the importance of restoring broken relationships, Father Anthony simply replied, "Of course, Christians have always known that."[2]

Thankfully, Kenneth didn't give up. He kept bringing up his desire for a conversation with Susan about the compatibility of EFT with the teachings of the Bible, and in a moment of weakness, Susan finally agreed. She said later, "I don't know why I agreed to it. I thought it was pointless, and I believed it just wouldn't matter."[3]

When Kenneth arrived at Susan's training center in Canada, the conversation lasted for three days. Kenneth brought up verse after verse about the importance of love and restoring relationships, and after many long hours of thoughtful discussion, Susan finally came to see that "it would be difficult to find an institution more committed to the task of reconciliation and the restoration of loving relationships than the church."[4]

Susan was familiar with the verses Kenneth brought up. She had heard them all before. But she had never had them presented to her in this way. Now they made perfect sense to her. Just like Father Anthony, Kenneth was talking to her about the importance of relationships, not rules. This was the message of Christianity, and this was the message of her life's work.

The result of that conversation with Kenneth is that Susan agreed to publish a book specifically directed toward helping Christians, *Created for Connection: The Hold Me Tight Guide for Christian Couples*. In that book she says, "I now have a spiritual perspective on this and can see bonding relationships as echoing what the Bible describes as 'becoming one' with a loved one."[5] And while this transformation is a wonderful thing, the religious humiliation of her childhood still has its effect. Today Susan describes herself as more of a seeker than someone who has found her spiritual home. She is an intellectually honest pilgrim on her path toward God. But she just as quickly says that her appreciation for the teachings found in the Bible has also been renewed.

Our attempts to correct others with shame and humiliation does far more damage than any good that could ever come out of it. Dr. Susan Johnson is just one of many examples of this fact. But I am not blaming the Catholic Church here, because then I would be guilty of the very thing that I am saying we shouldn't do. It is just as notable to point out that the humility of Father Anthony produced far more good in Susan's life than any teaching she ever received. Humility is having the confidence to know who you are and choosing to serve others out of love. Humility is not passivity or weakness. It is the most powerful way to inspire others from within. When Jesus told his followers, "As I have loved you, so you must love one another" (John 13:34), he wasn't giving them a formula for sentimentality so everyone would feel good. He was instructing them on how to live the most powerful life possible with others.

HUMILITY IS NOT PASSIVITY

We often speak of passive people as being humble. They don't make waves, and they try not to upset people, so we give them the benefit of the doubt by calling them humble. But humility is not the absence of action, it is the presence of love. Humility doesn't come from a lack of self-confidence or low self-esteem. No one really respects people like that, and their passivity doesn't connect us to them. We view them as harmless and ineffectual, and the truth is we are not impacted by them much at all. Rather than insulting them by pointing out their inefficacy, we simply call them humble.

Another way of understanding the difference between passivity and humility is by looking at the distinction between being nice and being kind. Nice people avoid hurting other people's feelings. This is not a bad thing, but when it comes at the price of our own honesty, being nice can be inauthentic. Too often nice people deny their own feelings to accommodate the feelings of others. When this happens, being nice is being dishonest, and it usually means being dishonest with yourself. To keep the peace with others, nice people often won't admit how they truly feel even to themselves. Looking at it this way, I don't think Jesus was trying to be nice very often. He was never dishonest about how he felt, with himself or other people, and he said a number of things that the religious people of his day thought were not very nice at all.

People who are nice often feel they cannot express their true feelings out of fear that doing so will cause a conflict or result in their rejection. The reason they push their true feelings out of conscious awareness in order to please others is because they are motivated by shame. Their fear is that if they remove their cloak of disguise that protects them from being truly seen, they will be exposed to ridicule or rejection like the Elephant Man, and we all know what happened to him.

However, I do believe that Jesus was always *kind*. Kindness doesn't require denial; it requires confidence. Being kind means considering the feelings of others while remaining honest about how you feel at the same time. Being kind might mean setting aside your feelings out of compassion for the feelings of others, and choosing to put their needs ahead of yours if the situation calls for it. But to be truly kind, you have to be able to be honest, at least with yourself.

When Jesus said, "If anyone slaps you on the right cheek, turn to them the other cheek also" (Matthew 5:39), he was not instructing us to be nice. This is far from an argument for passivity; it is an example of the power of love. He did not say, "When someone slaps you on the right cheek, cast your eyes to the ground, cower with humiliation, and turn and walk away." No, he was saying to stand your ground and refuse to believe that violence is stronger than love. Jesus was teaching us that love is stronger than hatred, and that if you stand up to haters and demand that they take your life of love and humility seriously, you will discover the full power of love. To have this type of humility, you must be absolutely convinced of your worthiness. Humility is not the absence of action; it is the manifestation of the power of love in relationships. Jesus was saying, "If someone slaps you out of hatred, you stand there and love them to death if need be." And he certainly wasn't telling us to do anything that he wasn't willing to do himself. You can overcome others with the power of kindness, but the process might not look very nice.

HUMILITY AND GUILT

Professor Tangney's research has uncovered some powerful truths. The first one is that shame-proneness is related to all kinds of psychological problems. If you are shame-prone, each twinge of shame will not just be a temporary feeling of inadequacy for you; it will signal an instantaneous feeling of defectiveness that makes you feel that who you are is worthless and there is no other way you are ever going to feel. Shame-proneness is habitual, automatic, and very damaging.

But the second revelation that Professor Tangney came to in her years of research is that the feeling of guilt is actually not a bad thing. While shame-proneness is associated with all kinds of psychological problems, guilt, and even guilt-proneness, is not. What I called neurotic guilt earlier, or guilt that has shame attached to it, does cause people problems, but the shame is what is doing the damage. Interestingly, guilt by itself is often a good thing.

Tangney found in her research that shame-free guilt is unrelated to psychological problems and actually helps people to be more empathic, to deal with their anger in more constructive ways, and to have more benevolent interpersonal relationships.[6] Tangney found that shame is related to depression, but guilt is not. She found that guilt-prone people are more likely to go to college, have fewer suicide attempts, use drugs less, get arrested less often, have fewer sexual partners in life, and practice safe sex more often.

The key to understanding why guilt-proneness produces these positive effects is that guilt is the bad feeling we get when we have done something wrong. We are focused on the bad thing we did, not the bad person we are. Focusing on the bad thing we did turns our attention to the problem at hand and motivates us to want to do something to fix it. Guilt motivates us to take action to repair damaged relationships or make amends. So when guilt-prone people feel bad about something that happened, they are likely to be more empathic about the other person's feelings. And even if guilt-prone people do get angry, they are more likely to use their anger constructively, for they feel bad about what they did rather than about who they are. Shame, on the other hand, causes people to focus on their worthlessness, which makes them defensive and more likely to fly off the handle in destructive ways.

Shame-free guilt produces humility. Feeling bad about what you did motivates you to restore any broken relationship that resulted from it. You are able to see the value in others because you are not having any doubts about your own worth as a result of what just happened. You don't have to be defensive because you don't have anything to hide, as you would if you felt shame. The apostle Paul was getting at this when he said, "Do not think of yourself more highly than you ought, but think of yourself with sober judgment" (Romans 12:3). He didn't say we should think of ourselves as less than others, but he instructed us to have an accurate perspective of who we are. Trying to pretend that you are superior to others is defensive and destructive. If you ever do that, you are probably feeling shame and trying to hide behind a paper-thin wall of self-centeredness. Confident people are free to be humble, and they don't have to view others as being beneath them. They can easily feel guilt over what they have done and compassion for anyone they have hurt in the process. This type of shame-free guilt leads us naturally to humility and empowers us to have the capacity for sober judgment in times of need.

I need to reiterate that guilt can get mixed with shame, and that can cause problems. You probably know people who are very guilt-prone and therefore are never really happy about anything. This is neurotic guilt, and if you look very closely at these people, you will always find them struggling with shame. This is actually closer to low self-esteem, which has nothing to do with humility. People with true humility experience shame-free guilt, which allows them to feel a sense of worth in the midst of negative events and to have the capacity to repair damaged relationships in the process.

The ideal would be to be a person who is able to experience the feelings of shame and guilt periodically, but even if you are a guilt-prone person, this doesn't have to be a problem. If you habitually respond to negative events with shame-free guilt, you are someone who cares about the feelings of others and feels bad when bad things happen. What's important here is that you don't get a painful feeling of worthlessness about your sense of self; you are just feeling bad about what happened. That is a tricky distinction but a valuable one.

"THIS IS MY COMMAND: LOVE EACH OTHER" (JOHN 15:17)

Jesus was relentless about the importance of love. He was very clear that dogma doesn't heal us; relationships with God and one another do. But to live this way requires humility. When trying to describe theological truth with your words, you will need to have the humility that you might not be saying it quite right. What you will never get wrong is that God's love is the most powerful force in the universe. God created it as the glue that connects us to him and the glue that holds us together here on earth.

Paul reminds us "Now I know in part; then I shall know fully" (1 Corinthians 13:12). I know that absolute truth exists, but I can only describe it from my limited perspective. Paul was not a relativist, because he did not teach that all truth is relative. Some things are right, and other things are wrong. But what he was getting at is that our ability to understand things with our human minds is limited, so try as we might, we will only get it partly right with our imperfect human capacities.

I think we can learn a lesson from Sister Mary Ellen. Her lack of humility and liberal use of humiliation was a formula that alienated one of the most brilliant psychological minds of our generation from the truths of Scripture for decades, and almost caused her to never open a Bible again, ever. Spirituality without humility is toxic. Again, before we blame Sister Mary Ellen we need to have some humility ourselves here. Have you ever engaged in a discussion about the Bible or issues of faith with someone in a way that made you come across as lacking humility? Were you so confident that you were right that you forgot to consider how you were making the other person feel? Is it possible that you may have embarrassed someone in your zeal to convince that person of the truth and possibly even humiliated him or her? You can win the argument and lose the person if you lack humility.

So let's also take a lesson from Father Anthony. He was completely confident that he knew the truth about God, and he was always sad that Susan refused to come back to church. But he had the humility to love and serve her despite their disagreements. Who was to say what God was doing in her heart? Only God knew. What Susan knew is that she felt loved by Father Anthony, and Father Anthony knew that the love she experienced came from God. He didn't need to demand that she have all the correct theological answers to his questions, and he wasn't going to humiliate her with Hail Marys if she couldn't get the answers right.

I am reminded of a question the internationally renowned biblical scholar George Eldon Ladd asked during the last course he ever taught on New Testament theology, which I had the honor of attending when I was in seminary. Given his lifelong commitment to precise biblical exegesis, I was almost surprised to hear him challenge us with a question he asked himself when debating other scholars with whom he strongly disagreed: "How wrong can a person be in their head but still be right in their heart?" That's something to think about.

Having confidence and humility is important. They go hand in hand. Humility is never passive, and sometimes it may not look very nice, but it is always based on a secure sense of worthiness and confidence that God's love heals us of our deepest wounds. You may never see the fruits of your impact on others in life, but if you approach others with humility, you can trust that you are going about your relationships in the most powerful way possible.

CHAPTER FIVE

Jesus and Self-Esteem

Adam and Eve were created for the purpose of joyful relationships with God and each other. They were naked with no shame in the Garden. It's hard even to imagine that kind of vulnerability, completely without embarrassment or awkward self-consciousness. But the truth is, that is how we all were created to live.

Humans *play* more than any other animal on earth. From childhood through adulthood, we come together to work hard as a community far beyond what any other animal is capable of doing, and we get together with coordinated efforts to play just as hard as we work. Psychologists believe that is where we develop what we call our *theory of mind*. This means that through playing and having fun with one another, we develop the capacity to realize that we have beliefs and feelings that we like to think of as our own, which helps us to realize that other people have them as well. You develop the concept of "making up your own mind" by bouncing ideas off other people who also think and feel, and the major way we do that is through play. You may not have thought about it this way before, but being joyful and having fun is not just a luxury or goofing around; it is essential to developing a healthy sense of self. This proves it: God really does have a sense of humor.

Adam and Eve were *valuable* to God. They were the pinnacle of his creation, and the Bible tells us that as soon as they were complete, "God saw all that he had made, and it was very good" (Genesis 1:31). God clearly took great joy in simply having them around.

But that was not all. Adam and Eve were also *useful* to God. God instructed Adam to name all the animals, and then he told Adam and Eve to rule over everything that he had made and to be fruitful and fill the earth with more humans so that they could reign over it. The Bible tells us, "The LORD God took the man and put him in the Garden of Eden to work it and take care of it" (Genesis 2:15). We were designed for both work and play from the very beginning of time. So two aspects of our relationship with God right from the start were that we were valuable and useful.

SELF-ESTEEM

Self-esteem is a concept that is very misused, but addressing it in any conversation about guilt and shame is essential. Basically, self-esteem is the feeling of value that comes from competence and secure attachments. False self-esteem masquerades as true self-esteem, but that is like comparing self-centeredness to self-confidence. The former does damage to your relationships, and the latter helps them improve.

When Jesus said, "For all those who exalt themselves will be humbled, and those who humble themselves will be exalted" (Luke 14:11), he was not saying that everyone who views themselves as less than others in this life will get a greater reward in the next one. No, he was cutting to the core of the dysfunctional nature of self-centeredness, and how everyone who lives this way is undermining any true power they might have with others. Sure, selfish people can get things for themselves and take advantage of others, but no one will respect them or look up to them for it. Only the truly confident person who has a secure sense of love and belonging is free to be humble; and all those who live this way are the ones that have a lasting impact on others. They will be the ones that others respect and look up to because they are living in the way God created us to be. False self-esteem is selfish and unattractive. True self-esteem is confidence that draws others toward us because we value the image of God in each of us. This is who we were designed to be: created beings who have value to God and one another.

To have true self-esteem, you must have both of the aspects Adam and Eve had in their relationships with God in the Garden: You must feel both useful and valuable. You must have a sense of accomplishment, and having those accomplishments recognized by others is crucial, for their affirmation makes you feel useful in life. But to have your self-esteem rounded out, you must also feel valuable independent of your accomplishments. You must feel that you have value for being who you are, and that your relationships are secure because of it. This is not something you can earn through working at it; it is something you feel because you have inherent worth as a human being created in God's image. Some people have described this as the difference between being and doing. You must feel good about being who you are, and you must feel good about doing what you do. Both are essential.

Because of the overemphasis on accomplishments in previous generations, some people have made the mistake of thinking that feeling valuable is all that matters when it comes to self-esteem. They say things like, "We are human *beings*, not human *doings*," emphasizing the significance of feeling valued over feeling useful. They believe that everyone should receive a trophy for participation in life, and that success doesn't matter—only having inherent worth does. But this idea is wrongheaded. If your parents told you that you are perfect just the way you are and they had no expectations that you accomplish anything in life, you will have only half of what is needed for healthy self-esteem (and may even feel narcissistically entitled to things that you don't deserve). You must also have confidence in what you can *do* to feel a well-rounded sense of self-esteem.

Of course, it is just as damaging to place all your emphasis in parenting on accomplishments and fail to communicate that children have value simply because God made them. This is a problem with which we all are familiar, and it results in people who can be very successful at work but struggle terribly in their personal relationships. Or, as Jesus said of our relationship with God, "What good is it for someone to gain the whole world, yet forfeit their soul?" (Mark 8:36). Overemphasizing usefulness is a mistake.

So a healthy sense of self comes from a balance of both usefulness and valuableness. That is not a problem. A problem does arise, however, when your sense of self becomes colored by shame.

DEVELOPING A SENSE OF SELF

Your sense of self and your feelings of shame develop at the same time. From the very first days of life, you were reaching out to connect to others, long before you had any concept of what you were doing. If someone responded to you, you developed a positive sense of self. If no one did, you didn't. We now know that infants just three days old will turn toward their own mother's milk in preference to someone else's milk.[1] Relationships matter to us from the start. Scientists tell us we are hardwired to seek out secure relationships; the Bible tells us we were created to do so.

Just recently neuroscientists have discovered the existence of *mirror neurons* in the brain.[2] If you observe someone doing something, such as drinking a cup of coffee, the neurons in your brain will fire as if you are drinking a cup of coffee yourself. Your brain will "mirror" the brain of the person you are observing. And what is more, the neurons in your brain will continue to fire along a path that anticipates what the person you are observing will do next. Without any logical reasoning at all (because the rational part of the brain is not involved in this process), within fractions of a second your brain reads the intentions of the person you are observing. If they are feeling something, you feel it. If they are about to do something, you anticipate it. Neuroscientists believe mirror neurons to be the biological basis for empathy, and we are hardwired this way from birth. Empathy is instantaneous and automatic.

This amazing discovery illustrates just how fundamentally relational we are as human beings. You can't help it; your brain is hardwired to respond to other people without even thinking about it. We "read" the intentions of others and respond neurologically almost instantly. You just *think* you made up your own mind about wanting that cup of coffee, but the truth is, if other people around you are drinking coffee, you are prompted to follow right along. It appears we are more *tribal*, or a group-thinking species, than we realized.

I need to offer a word of caution here. Even though you are reading the intentions of others, you are still *interpreting* what you are seeing. Your mirror neurons are not mirroring the exact same thing that is going on in the other person's head; they are mirroring what you believe you are seeing. In other words, you may think you know the intentions of the other person, but you may not be reading them exactly right. This explains many of the marital fights I observe in my counseling office. People are often *certain* that they know what the other person meant by what that person said, and they believe the other person is just not being honest by refusing to own up to it. But even though we are hardwired to try to read the intentions of others, no one has a 100 percent success rate at getting them right. The next time you get in a fight with someone you know very well, don't be so certain that you knew what their intentions were when they said that thing that upset you so much. You were hardwired to read their intentions, but you are hardheaded if you think you are always right.

One of the most dramatic examples of our relational nature is an experiment conducted by Professor Ed Tronick at the University of Massachusetts called the Still Face Experiment.[3] This experiment has been conducted many times in many different situations, and the results are always the same. Professor Tronick took infants as young as four months old and had their mothers sit directly in front of them for three minutes. First the mother responded normally to the child. If the child smiled, the mother smiled. If the mother looked at something, the infant did the same.

Then they instructed the mothers to hold very still with an expressionless face. In every case, the infant made repeated attempts to get the mother to respond in the usual reciprocal pattern to which they were both accustomed. The infant smiled, but the mother didn't respond. The infant pointed at something, but the mother remained motionless. Within seconds all the infants first protested, feeling something was wrong. Then when everything failed, all the infants withdrew and turned their faces away from their mothers with hopeless facial expressions. Watching videos of this is painful (you can easily find several online). We are born to seek out relationships, and we feel bad if we reach out and no one is there.

The Still Face Experiment has a couple of interpretations. The most popular is that we are hardwired to seek secure attachments, and we become disorganized when we fail to find them. Someone has also suggested that the reason the infants fall into despondency is because they are seeking a sense of efficacy. The child wants to elicit a response from the familiar face staring back, and when repeated attempts fail, the automatic response is one of discouragement. No matter how you interpret it, this failure to receive the responsiveness that is so clearly needed is the beginning of shame. We are made by God to seek a relationship with someone outside of ourselves, bigger than us, who is seeking to have a relationship with us too. And if we do not find it, we feel bad. Whether it is the loss of secure attachment or the loss of the ability to make a difference in other people's lives, you will feel worthless if no one is there when you reach out, and this bad feeling is the prototype of what will later become the feeling of shame.

The sobering conclusion of the Still Face Experiment is that it doesn't take an abusive parent to create feelings of shame in a child. The mothers were not scolding their children or mocking them, and they certainly weren't trying to humiliate them. They simply were not responding. The lack of responsiveness was all that was needed for their children to fall into hopelessness. And this reaction has been observed in people of all ages. This should make you think about every relationship you have today, especially your closest ones. Your sense of self develops as you read the responses on the faces of the people around you, and feelings of shame develop if you don't get anything back.

OVERCOMPENSATING FOR
UNDERRESPONSIVENESS

So what do we do when we don't get what we need? Well, one of the things we do is overcompensate. If you were created for joyful relationships with God and others, and you have not received the responsiveness you need to feel joyful, you start to feel shame that causes you to doubt your value and usefulness to God and others. This is not a good thing.

Feelings of guilt and shame are natural regulators of our relationships. If we feel bad about something we have done, we are motivated to repair any damage we may have caused to our relationships. If we feel less than someone else momentarily, this can be helpful information to guide us to appropriate action. But if we fail to get the responsiveness we need for too long, we develop a damaging unconscious belief about our sense of self. Now we no longer feel the momentary feeling of shame, but we develop a shame-prone response to negative events that perpetuates the belief that we are worthless in a way that we come to believe cannot be changed.

If you develop shame-proneness, you will probably form defensive strategies to protect yourself from feelings that are too painful to tolerate. You will not be able to feel confident in your value to God and others, so you will have to find some way to compensate for this. One strategy is to overestimate your value and insist that you are more than good enough for everything, and probably superior to others if everyone would just be honest about it. Psychologists call this *narcissism*. The odd thing about narcissistic people is that they know they are narcissistic and they just don't care. They see their narcissism as a personality trait, like extroversion. It's just the way they are. They are better than others, and they can't help it. But every psychologist will tell you that at the very core of narcissism you will *not* find someone who loves himself or herself too much or has too much self-esteem; instead, you will find agonizing feelings of shame. If I have piqued your interest here, you will be glad to know that I have a lot more to say about this in the chapter on narcissism.

SELF-RIGHTEOUSNESS

A particularly obnoxious manifestation of this overestimation of one's worth is self-righteousness. Jesus had a lot to say about religious narcissism. He was always saying things like, "Be careful not to practice your righteousness in front of others to be seen by them. If you do, you will have no reward from your Father in heaven" (Matthew 6:1). What he knew but didn't have the psychological terminology to say is that self-righteousness is caused by shame-proneness. It is exactly because you *doubt* your valuableness that you must insist that you have greater value than others. Your religious practices can never make you more righteous. In fact, the term *righteous* was used throughout the Old Testament as a term for people who had a *right relationship* with God. It had nothing to do with superspiritual religious practices. Self-righteousness is not a manifestation of superspirituality; it is an overcompensation for hidden feelings of shame.

Toward the end of Jesus's earthly ministry, the disciples started to get excited about what was about to happen next. They misunderstood Jesus's mission and were holding out for some sort of new political system they thought he was going to create, one that would correct all the injustices of the current governmental rule. They bickered among themselves about who was the greatest and who would be most likely to be in a position of power when the new world order came about. I'm sure that Jesus had to roll his eyes when he said, "The kings of the Gentiles lord it over them; and those who exercise authority over them call themselves Benefactors. But you are not to be like that. Instead, the greatest among you should be like the youngest, and the one who rules like the one who serves" (Luke 22:25-26). I guess we should be comforted by the fact that even the people who knew Jesus personally still struggled with shame and self-righteousness. A lack of faith or spiritual maturity is not the problem; rather, the problem is unacknowledged shame.

The problem with self-righteousness is not simple. The church has a built-in contradiction that fosters shame because we get together as a group of people who are intentionally trying not to do shameful things, but this is the same group of people to whom we are supposed to expose our shame so that we might be healed.[4] I think you can see the difficulty here.

MARY AND MARTHA

I believe we have been too hard on Martha. Remember the story about Mary and Martha in the Bible where Mary is sitting at Jesus's feet and Martha is running around trying to get the meal ready? Martha ends up getting frustrated with Mary and blurts out, "Lord, don't you care that my sister has left me to do the work by myself? Tell her to help me!" (Luke 10:40). Jesus tells her to calm down and get her priorities straight. I think he was pointing out to Martha that she was trying to substitute usefulness for valuableness, and you can't really do that. Martha wasn't doing anything wrong by trying to be useful, but her criticism of Mary grew out of her inability to see the value in just wanting to be with Jesus. We all are somewhat to blame for Martha's kind of thinking. We constantly stress in the church that good people do good things, so it is very easy to develop the belief that doing good deeds is the proof that someone is righteous. I mean, you will know a good tree by its fruit, right?

THE SINGLES RETREAT

Many years ago, I was invited to be the guest speaker for a singles retreat that a church was holding at a ski resort. I had never skied before, but I did speak to singles groups at churches often. Since their singles minister, Rick, was a friend of mine, I accepted the invitation. The group was made up of mostly middle-aged divorced people who were courageously trying to face their marital failures and support one another rather than drifting away from church because they were too embarrassed to show their faces there anymore. Rick even had a banner made that he proudly displayed at each meeting, announcing: God Loves Divorced People. This was a twist on Malachi 2:16, which some translations of the Bible record God as saying, "I hate divorce." Rick was declaring that God may hate divorce, but he loves divorced people. I liked his attitude.

I won't go into how difficult the skiing was for me, but by the end of the day when the group gathered for the lecture part of the retreat, we all were pretty hungry and tired. These were good people, honestly trying to recover from the devastation of divorce and genuinely asking God and the Christian community to help them do it. As we transitioned from our meal together to the part of the evening that I was supposed to lead, I couldn't help but notice an interesting thing. All of the men dutifully moved into the seating area where we were instructed to go to hear my lecture. But only about half of the women responded to that instruction. As I looked to the back of the room where the kitchen area was, I saw a number of women standing around looking for something to do. They couldn't help it—they were Marthas, and they couldn't even force themselves to be different than what they were. Rick asked everyone to move into the seating area several times, but these women were just too uncomfortable to go there.

I know I am being terribly politically incorrect in pointing this out, but I am only telling you what I observed. I knew these women. They had all raised children, tried to be good wives to their husbands, and worked hard to be good Christian women all of their lives. But now here they were, more than halfway through their lives, alone and trying to figure out how they were going to rebuild their identities. The women who had maintained careers during their marriages were comfortable enough to leave the kitchen area, but the ones who had given up their professions for a different calling weren't. Working full-time *inside* the home was the major job qualification on their résumés. What were they supposed to do now? Who were they supposed to be at this point in their lives when none of them had expected to end up here?

If your husband leaves you for what you did, you will feel guilty for that. But if he leaves you for who you are, well then, the major thing you are going to feel is shame. I could make the same point about men (and I have elsewhere), but an extremely common response to shame in marriage is to overcompensate for not feeling valued by trying to be useful instead. The problem is, it doesn't work. No amount of performance will ever make up for not feeling valued. You will receive recognition and appreciation for being useful, and those are good things. But you will never feel valued simply by making yourself useful to others. You cannot overcome your shame by overcompensating with usefulness. It doesn't work.

Not feeling appreciated for what you do hurts your self-esteem, but not feeling valued for who you are is even more crushing. In many marriages both men and women try to overcompensate for not feeling valued by overemphasizing their usefulness. But this trade-off ends in frustration for both. He will eventually complain that he never feels appreciated for how hard he tries but still gets told that it isn't good enough, or she will become more and more critical of him in response to feeling ignored and unloved (except for when he is interested in sex). This lack of emotional responsiveness from a spouse erodes self-esteem and eventually lays down the unconscious belief that your very sense of self is worthless whenever anything negative happens in the relationship. And it doesn't necessarily take years of vicious fighting to create shame in your spouse. Tronick's Still Face Experiments have proven that for us. Sometimes not getting any emotional response back from your partner at all is enough to leave you with a stinging feeling of shame. Shame-prone marriages result in marital conflicts that never seem to get resolved and self-images that grow more and more negative. In other words, one of the biggest culprits in unhappy marriages is unhealed shame.

I want to stress again that I'm not blaming the women at the retreat for being Marthas. We all have contributed to their dilemma. We created a culture of expectations and an emphasis on performance as the solution to our difficulties. And I especially don't want to blame the gender roles that these women agreed on with their partners as creating the problem. There is nothing wrong with agreed-on gender roles, traditional or not. Staying home to raise children is an honorable and wonderful life choice. But in any marriage, if you try to substitute usefulness for valuableness, you will eventually have a problem with shame that needs to be addressed. To feel good, both spouses in any relationship must feel useful and valuable.

More Useful Than Valuable

If you feel more useful than valuable, examining how you feel about your sense of self may be helpful. In many cases the underlying issue is a gradually evolving shame-proneness that developed over many years. Maybe you were raised to get your sense of self-worth from performance, or perhaps you have lived in a marriage where most of what you got back from your bids for emotional attunement were expressionless "still faces" looking back at you. But no matter how you got here, if you are trying to get love by becoming useful to others, it is not likely to work very well.

When the apostle Paul said, "Love is the fulfillment of the law" (Romans 13:10), he was making a profound statement about how to have a genuine relationship with God, or anyone else for that matter.

Living by the letter of the law will not get you where you want to be. There is nothing wrong with the law; it's just that the law cannot make you feel loved. Only a relationship in which you feel valued can do that. Paul was saying that you cannot earn your value in God's sight, and it doesn't work with other people either. No one can be obedient or useful enough to merit value. The only basis for a fulfilling relationship with anyone is because you view that person as valuable. And few things in life will heal a person of shame more than that.

Psychiatrist Curt Thompson says that love and shame are always competing for our attention.[5] You cannot overcome your shame by yourself, so working harder at being more productive or useful will never do it. The feeling of shame came from your relationships with others, and the healing of it will only come from there as well. But instead of trying to be more useful to others, you will need to be more vulnerable to them. Shame makes you believe a lie about yourself—that you are defective and worthless. So your shame will make you want to hide; the opposite of what love wants you to do.

If you feel more useful than valuable, you are going to have to come out of the kitchen. You and Martha have done a lot of good work in there, and you have many more good and useful things to do ahead of you. But you have an imbalance in your life that needs to be addressed, and you can't keep doing the same thing over and over again expecting a different result.[6] Your shame wants you to work harder at being more useful to others. Your hope is that someday they will see your value and turn to you with all the love you have needed for years. But this is not likely to happen.

On the other hand, you could recognize that the problem is not that other people are just too thickheaded to see how valuable you are as a result of how hard you have been working all these years. They do see how productive you have been, and they are grateful for how useful you are. But you don't need more recognition for your usefulness; you need unmerited love to affirm your value. These are two different things. *They* may not be the problem; *you* might be trying to solve it with the wrong solution.

PATHOLOGICAL ACCOMMODATION

Psychoanalysts have a term for people who are trying to solve the problem of not feeling valued with trying to be more useful—*pathological accommodation*.[7] There is generally nothing wrong with trying to be an accommodating person. Setting aside your needs for the needs of those you love from time to time is a good thing. But when you do this because you are motivated by shame, eventually no one benefits from the process.

Accommodating the needs of others because you love them makes you feel good about yourself. This kind of self-sacrifice is simply being a loving person. But accommodating others because you are shame-prone is a different thing. Sacrifice out of low self-esteem is not sacrifice out of love. The primary motivation here is fear, not love, and fear and love do not go well together.

Psychoanalysts have identified that this type of sacrifice is motivated by shame and painful feelings of worthlessness that you fear will be exposed, so you insist that the needs of the other person are more important than yours under the guise that you are simply being a considerate person. This is not a manifestation of love but is a selfish motivation to hide underlying shame. Pathological accommodation is driven by shame-proneness, and this is not what Jesus had in mind when he said, "The Son of Man did not come to be served, but to serve" (Matthew 20:28). Jesus did not for one moment ever doubt his value, and his life of self-sacrifice had nothing to do with feelings of hidden shame. He was completely confident in his ultimate worth as the Son of God, and because of that solid sense of self, he was free to serve others out of love. This was his model for how we should live our lives as well.

You may not have the confidence of Jesus Christ, and you don't need to. You can simply follow his life as an example. You can be self-sacrificing from a place of love, and you will feel both useful and valuable to God and others. If self-sacrificing gets out of balance in your life, you will have a clue as to where to look to make some adjustments. Service out of fear is not the same thing as service out of love. If you are feeling more useful than valuable, you are eventually going to feel unappreciated and disappointed in other people. You are being self-sacrificing and yet others just don't seem to have the same giving attitude as you. If you are feeling this way, the problem may not be that other people are ungrateful; it could be that you are being motivated by your own shame.

CHAPTER SIX

Resentment: The Deadly Weapon That Backfires

Resentment is deadly. I mean it. We have enough research now to know that if you get caught up in resentment, it can follow you around for years, eating you up from the inside and causing all kinds of emotional and physical problems. Resentment will cost you much more than it will cost the person you resent. And yet it is still difficult to release. We love it, but it hates us.

First, let me say that the problem with resentment is not anger per se. The apostle Paul gives us clear instructions: "In your anger do not sin" (Ephesians 4:26). So anger itself is not a sin, but what we do with it certainly can be, and probably so often that Paul needed to give us a word of warning. Know that *anger is simply energy to solve a problem.* If you use it as it is intended, you solve the problem and the anger goes away. I think Paul knew this, because he finished Ephesians 4:26 with "Do not let the sun go down while you are still angry." Precisely. Anger is a burst of energy designed to get at the root of a problem (something underneath the anger), and once that problem is correctly addressed, you can sleep well that night. This is how things are supposed to be.

Okay, let's add to this that God created you to be a moral person. You have a conscience (unless you are a psychopath as we discussed earlier), and you know the difference between right and wrong. This being the case, if you witness something that is morally wrong, you will have a reaction. If the moral wrongdoing is bad enough, you will even very likely get angry. This type of anger we call *righteous indignation*, which is the natural response of a moral person to immoral wrongdoing. Immorality should make you angry because anger is energy to solve a problem, and in the face of immoral wrongdoing, you are motivated by your anger to intervene. Your conscience stimulates you to defend goodness against evil in the world. That's how God made us. This use of anger is not only *not* a sin; it is the godly reaction of a moral person made in the image of God. *Some* anger is from God.

Because anger is God's own reaction to immoral wrongdoing, he has been moved to anger many times over the course of history. At times he responded with punishment to correct the situation (Romans 1:18). This type of punishment (or retribution) is the moral response to immoral behavior on which all societies are based. Justice requires good people to stop bad behavior, and punishment is the way we do it. Bad behavior is punished to protect the good, and sometimes our anger is necessary to motivate us to do it. This can be very difficult, but it is still good and necessary for imperfect human beings to live together. In these ways, anger is a powerful emotion to motivate us to take care of difficult problems. Used correctly, it is a good thing.

WHAT IS RESENTMENT?

So far, so good. Anger has its place in the universe, and sometimes it is a good and necessary thing to help decent human beings live well together. But resentment is different from righteous indignation. This is a different class of anger altogether. Resentment is *the response to feeling demeaned.*[1] We don't resent tornadoes. We resent people. A tornado can hurt you, but only another person can make you feel demeaned. Resentment motivates you to retaliate and balance the scales that have been tipped in the wrong direction by someone who believes they are entitled to mistreat you. Resentment is the angry response to feeling demeaned, and it is your personal attempt to defend your self-worth. You are personally under attack, and resentment is your weapon to retaliate.

Resentment is such an intense feeling that it can take over your life. Wars have been fought, people have been murdered, and lives have been destroyed because of it. And here is the key to understanding why resentment is so powerful and enduring, and why some people will sacrifice their lives for it: The demeaning action of the person who triggered your resentment has *caused you to doubt your self-worth.* At this point the problem is not what other people think of you; it's that you have painful feelings of inferiority yourself. That's right. The heart of resentment isn't the moral need to balance the ethical scales of injustice—it's shame. You have been demeaned, and now you fear that your worth has been diminished. This throws you into the grips of painful feelings of fear that not only have you been hurt, but your worth has been lessened as well. Deep within, you may even have the terrible fear that you deserved to be mistreated (this is usually not a conscious thought, but something much deeper), and this stimulates a piercing rage that makes you protest loudly that this is not true. The reason resentment is so powerful is not because you have an issue with the other person; it is because you have a terribly painful issue with yourself.

Resentment is the anger you feel for being made to feel inadequate. If you were demeaned in a way that has diminished your self-worth (in your own mind), now you are dealing with agonizing feelings of shame. And as you know, no one wants to feel shame. So what does your resentment make you want to do? Focus your anger on the other person. That person is the one who acted badly; that person is the one who is wrong; and that person is the one who should be feeling bad right now, not you. So your anger attempts to direct all the attention outward, toward the offender, in a desperate attempt to distract everyone away from the real source of your pain—your own shame.

To deal with such a scenario, you have to grasp the distinction between righteous indignation and resentment. This is not always easy to do because they can look exactly the same on the outside. Sometimes the only way you can tell resentment from righteous anger is by knowing what is going on in the person's heart who is feeling it. Or just as difficult, if you are the one feeling the resentment, you have to search your own heart to know exactly why you feel the way you do. Obviously, this is not a simple matter when you have been hurt.

Michael's Story

Michael and Emily wanted to get married while they were still in college and begin a perfect life together. They both felt fortunate to find the love of their lives at such a young age, and they wanted to start spending the rest of their lives together right away. Why wait when you have found *the one*? Michael felt as though he were the luckiest man in the world; and Emily felt as if she had met the man of her dreams.

Emily was very close to her family and talked to them regularly. She knew that Michael wasn't close to his family, but she didn't think much of it at first. She was aware that her sisters' husbands were all closer to her family than their own, so she just thought that was the way things worked. Women are closer to their families, and the men they marry just tend to get drawn into them. After all, women are more social than men anyway. Aren't they?

But now that they were considering getting married, Emily wanted to develop more of a relationship with Michael's family. She didn't think it would be a big deal, but she wanted to have a closer relationship with them, and she wanted her children to have a good relationship with their grandparents on both sides of the family.

"So, Michael," Emily said one evening. "I've been thinking about us making a trip to visit your family."

"Why?" Michael asked, tensing up a bit.

"Because I want us to be a family. All of us. Isn't that what we are talking about becoming, a family? You and I are not just getting married; we are joining our families. Don't you think?"

"We *are* a family," Michael said, getting defensive. "You and me. And I want to have kids after we graduate so we can make a family of our own. And we have your parents anyway. I love your parents, and well, mine are just too difficult. You know how I feel about all that."

"Actually"—Emily wasn't backing down—"I *don't* know how you feel about your parents. You never call them. And I've never met them. So, I would like to get to know them. Is that so wrong?"

"Look, Emily," Michael said, getting upset now. "You don't understand. My father would not be the kind of grandfather you would want for your children, or anybody's children. I think we would be better off if we just left well enough alone. I don't want him having any influence on you or our children. He doesn't deserve it. *That's* how I feel about it."

Emily had no idea that Michael's feelings were so strong about his father. She knew his parents were divorced, and she was aware that he avoided talking about them, but she didn't know the animosity

between Michael and his father was this strong. Michael, like a lot
of young men, was suffering from a bad relationship with his father.
Many adult men have either a distant or broken relationship with
their fathers, and they have no idea what to do about it. Most of
them just go on with their lives, never resolving their paternal pain
and suffering its effects. Some never develop close, trusting relationships with other men; some can't tolerate a mentoring relationship
that limits their professional success; and some have difficulty in
all intimate relationships because of a father-wound that was never
healed. Michael was one of these men, angry with his father, and he
had been for years.

Michael's parents divorced when he was nine. His father moved
away, and Michael didn't hear from him for almost ten years. Those
years were pretty rough for Michael. Explaining to the other kids
why his father was never around was embarrassing, and being the
kid whose father was never there for any of his sports competitions
really hurt. Whatever his explanation eventually was, to Michael it
meant only one thing: His dad didn't care. If a young boy's father
doesn't think his son is worth the time to show up for when he needs
his dad, the boy has a hard time not believing it's true.

Michael knew he was angry with his father, but he never gave
any thought to what his anger meant. He knew his father had abandoned him and his mother. He knew this was wrong, and it was
something Michael would never do. He loved Emily and wanted
to marry her to show her what a committed husband and father he
was going to be, and to prove to everyone that he was nothing like
his father. Good men keep their promises, Michael believed, not
like his father.

Fortunately, Emily wasn't going to let this go. She knew Michael's
relationship with his father was hurting him and that it was only a
matter of time before that hurt was going to affect her and her future

children as well. She convinced Michael to come for premarital counseling where we could bring this out into the open and deal with it. Michael really didn't want to come to therapy sessions, but he loved Emily so much that he was willing to come and talk about his feelings regarding his father.

Michael thought he was justified in being angry with his father, and he thought he was taking the higher moral ground in insisting that the man be restricted from having any impact on Emily or anyone he loved. His father was selfish and hurtful; why would he want that type of person around? While this seems logical, the real motivation for Michael's feelings didn't have much to do with logic or morality at all. Michael was doing what many people do when they have been hurt like this. He was trying to convert an emotional problem into a moral one. If we can't express our deep hurt in emotional terms, we *moralize* the feelings and express our hurt in ethical terms.

"He doesn't deserve it," he would say, or "What kind of man abandons his family?"

Michael tried to cast his feelings in moral terms to keep the focus on his father and his bad behavior. Who could object with the fact that his father did a bad thing? While this sounded good to Michael, it only served to keep him stuck. The resentment Michael felt toward his father was never going to change as long as he kept the focus of his anger on his father and what he did wrong. It was only through weeks of honest conversation that we were able to shift the focus off of his father's behavior and onto how Michael felt as a result of it. We never justified his father's bad behavior, but what we did do was take a vulnerable look at how Michael felt—not just about his father but about himself. Michael wasn't just angry at the moral injustice of men abandoning their families; he was furious because his father's abandonment of *him* left him feeling deep feelings of shame.

Michael's father wasn't there to parent him into adult manhood at the time in his life when he desperately needed it. Michael often felt insecure about whether he was "doing it right" as a young man. Was he throwing the ball right? Was he being a good son? Was he relating to girls in the right way? He was never sure, so as a result he was dragging around painful feelings of self-doubt about himself as a man, and for that he blamed his father. Michael resented his father, and he wasn't going to stop resenting him until he could get a grasp on why. The real roots of Michael's resentment didn't have to do with what his father did; it had to do with the doubts Michael had about his own worth as a man because of it. This was the real root of his resentment, and until this was acknowledged, he was never going to give it up.

Fortunately, young men in love are very motivated. Emily caught Michael at just the right time in his life to ask him to come to counseling and deal with feelings he never talked about. Shame kept secret rarely gets better. Happily, Michael began to open up about how he felt. Instead of angrily insisting that he was going to be nothing like his father, honestly talking about his doubts about himself as a husband and father had a paradoxical effect on Michael. Instead of making him feel more insecure (as he feared), he could see the respect in Emily's eyes for having the courage to be vulnerable, and that actually started to erase those years of self-doubt he had been carrying around. He could see that he *was* doing it right now, and that made him feel good, especially about himself as a man trying his best to love the woman in his life. Michael was getting at the real roots of his resentment toward his father, and that was setting him free.

The end of the story with Michael (and the beginning of his new life with Emily) was that he eventually was able to forgive his father. But you can't truly forgive someone unless you acknowledge what the person did that was wrong in the first place. We forgive someone *for* wrongdoing, not in spite of it. Most men just excuse their fathers, tolerate them, try to forget what they did, deny what they did, or even come to a place where they accept their fathers. All these things are good and necessary at times, but none of them are forgiveness. Forgiveness is the honest acknowledgment of wrongdoing and the vulnerable naming of any doubts about your self-worth that have resulted from feeling demeaned, and then making the choice to release yourself from resentment by forgiving the one who has harmed you. You decide not to return hurt for hurt, independent of whether the other person is even aware of your decision to forgive them. This is not excusing what happened or engaging in some form of naive denial about it. True forgiveness requires the courageous self-awareness to tell the truth about what happened, how you feel, and what you are choosing to do about it—forgive.

Jesus knew all of this. His psychologically brilliant teaching on forgiveness cuts right to the heart of the matter. He said, "Why do you look at the speck of sawdust in your brother's eye and pay no attention to the plank in your own eye?" (Matthew 7:3). He got it. He knew that the real root of resentment was not what the other person did, and it didn't really have much to do with her or him as a person either. Sure, what the other person did was bad, but that is only a speck compared to the plank you are carrying around causing you to resent that person. And Jesus knew that this was only a matter of perspective. As things look to you in your own eyes, you think you see the problem clearly, but as Michael found out, his plank was completely preventing him from seeing the real problem at all. Once you are able to see that the real problem you have is with yourself and not the other person, the possibility of genuine forgiveness is close at hand.

Michael was able to forgive his father, not out of some

superspiritual piety he achieved as a result of our sessions together. We ended our premarital counseling with him being the same imperfect but in-love man he was when we started. But he was able to grasp a deeper meaning from Jesus's teachings on forgiveness and apply them to his life more fully than he had been able to before. He no longer resented his father for being the imperfect man he was, he stopped getting upset when Emily brought up his father's name, and he even made plans for her to meet his father. Michael didn't want to spend the rest of his life resenting his father; he just didn't know how to deal with it. Vulnerably bringing his hidden feelings of shame out into the open helped him do that, and Emily couldn't be happier that he did.

Does Punishing People Help?

If we are going to talk about resentment, we need to say a few things about punishment as well. As I mentioned, some punishment is necessary because we live in an imperfect world. Punishment based on righteous indignation is morally just because God himself punished immorality in the Bible. This type of punishment is called retribution because it is the moral response to immoral actions. Its purpose is to defend good people and good laws from the immoral claim that some people make that they are superior to the rest of us and do not have to live within the same moral constraints as everyone else. Just societies cannot live without retribution, and justice is based on this fact. That is not to say that all crimes are punished equally, because they are not. But part of justice is to determine how a certain punishment should fit a particular crime. In any case some punishment is necessary for us to live well together.

Retribution, however, has nothing to do with resentment. True retribution may have some element of righteous indignation involved, as seen when moral people are angered by the wrong-doing of some criminals. But this righteous indignation is not a personal anger that is in defense of one's own self-worth. Righteous indignation might go so far as to stimulate a moral person to hate the crime that is committed, but it is not likely to cause that person to hate the individual who committed the crime. There is no self-doubt in the mind of the moral person that would cause that person to use resentment to defend against their self-worth that had been demeaned. If you have not been personally demeaned, you are not likely to have been caused to doubt your worth, and so you are able to punish wrongdoing without having any feelings of resentment toward the person receiving the punishment. Hopefully, most parenting is done in this fashion. You punish your children because you love them and want them to live within the bounds of good moral behavior, so you punish them to correct them, not because you resent them for acting out. Hopefully.

Life is not often that simple, however. In many cases people do feel demeaned by the immoral actions of others, and their desire to see that person punished is then caused by a mixture of emotions. Some of it is righteous indignation stimulating them to want to see justice carried out. They are angered by what was done, and they want to see things made right again. But some of what they feel is resentment toward the offending party, and they want that person to suffer not just because they want retribution for what was done but because they want *revenge*. Revenge is the anger you feel when you have been mistreated in such a way that you feel demeaned and are now driven by resentment to seek justice. On the one hand, you are motivated by your moral indignation toward injustice, but on the other hand, you are driven by your personal resentment to see the other person *brought down*. Retribution is a healthy response to wrongdoing; revenge is not.

Revenge does not make you simply want to make things right again; it makes you want to get even. You feel demeaned, and now you feel your worth has been degraded, and you just can't let it go. You are angered that the offending person feels entitled to act as they do, and now you are driven to balance the scales of personal worth that have been thrown out of balance. That person is not better than you, and you are not going to let them get away with acting as though they are. Revenge is not motivated by righteous indignation; it is motivated by resentment. Revenge is very interested in seeking punishment for wrongdoing, but not for moral reasons, because revenge is driven by shame.

In light of this information, understanding things like our country's penal system is confusing. We need punishment for society to work, but when retribution gets mixed up with revenge, the reasons we are punishing people gets very hard to determine. Perhaps you have seen this when someone is talking about some way in which they have been offended. What happened to them was clearly wrong, but the way in which they are talking about their desire to see the other person punished makes you uncomfortable. The offending party should be punished; you can agree with that. But the hatred that the victim has for the offender seems so intense that you have to wonder what else is going on. This is not just a desire for justice; it is a thirst for revenge. The tragedy here is that even if the victim does see punishment carried out, they are still very likely to continue hating the offender for years to come. When this type of revenge motivates a victim to seek punishment, who is the one who is continuing to be punished long after the sentence has been legally carried out? Revenge based on resentment backfires, and victims continue to suffer no matter what kind of punishment is doled out. Few people realize they are giving themselves a life sentence in a prison of hatred when they are driven by revenge, regardless of whether the offending parties they resent ever receive any form of punishment.

So when it comes to punishing people for wrongdoing, getting confused is easy. Do I want to see some form of retribution motivated by a desire for justice, or am I seeking revenge motivated by my resentment? It's often not easy to tell, but here's a clue: If you are seeking a personal feeling of satisfaction, one that will give you some delight that the offender has gotten what they deserve, you may be struggling with some feelings of resentment. Resentment comes from feeling demeaned, so it is personal. You don't just want things to be restored to the way they should be; you also want to cover over painful feelings of shame. If you are seeking justice, you don't particularly delight in seeing someone punished. You don't want them to suffer; you want them to be corrected. To make this even clearer, it is possible to forgive someone and still punish them. Your forgiveness releases you from your resentment, so you have no personal desire to see the other person harmed, but the moral laws of God and society still require justice to be served. You have no desire to see the other person in pain, but you do have a desire for justice, which is to see things made right. On the other hand, revenge wants to see perpetrators hurt because you are trying to distract yourself from your own hurt, the painful feelings of shame that no one wants to feel. The next time you are offended and trying to figure out whether some sort of punishment is needed, you would do well to search your heart to try to discover what is motivating you.

MERCY

Let's take things one step further. If justice is punishing people according to their crimes, what is mercy? Justice, by definition, punishes lesser crimes with lesser punishment. If you shoplift, you can expect a lesser punishment than if you murder someone; that only makes sense. But mercy is the decision to release someone from a punishment they deserve. This is different from justice and retribution, because the person you show mercy to deserves to be punished; you know it and they know it. You have every moral right to expect that they receive punishment, but you are deciding to dismiss the execution of their punishment as an unmerited act of grace on your part. They don't deserve it, but you choose to do it anyway. Your decision has nothing to do with them, the merits of their character, or their behavior. It only has to do with the kind of person you are. Mercy is a display of your character and is not based on the characteristics of the person to whom you choose to give it. When it comes to mercy, the question is not whether the other person deserves it; the question is whether you have the character to give it.

The Bible tells us that "judgment without mercy will be shown to anyone who has not been merciful. Mercy triumphs over judgment" (James 2:13). Okay, that's a stiff requirement. We are supposed to have the character to release people from the punishment they deserve, even though they have not earned it. But at the same time, I'm grateful that God himself is merciful, because I wouldn't want to stand before him and get the punishment I deserve. Nobody would.

James is saying that judging produces judging, and mercy produces mercy. The more you judge and demand justice, the more you are judged and will be subject to punishment yourself. This is not always a bad thing, but you certainly will have times in your life when you will need to receive mercy, release from the punishment you deserve. And the more you have the character to show mercy to others, the more it will be shown to you. The Greek word for mercy in this passage can be translated "compassionate forbearance shown toward an offender." This is not an example of justice motivated by moral character; it is an example of love. All of our lives would be less without it.

Showing mercy toward someone who has offended you is not easy. You may have to work at it for quite a while to find the strength to do it when the time comes. But even though it is difficult, it is not impossible to show mercy toward a wrongdoer; that is, unless you feel resentment. Resentment limits our ability to show mercy and blocks our ability to show compassion. It erects a wall within us that keeps us stuck. Nothing gets in, and not much gets out. Resentment is the illusion that we are protecting ourselves from further harm, but the truth is we are harming ourselves every day we allow it to exist in us. You may be distancing yourself from a hurtful person with your bitter resentment toward them, but you are pushing down your shame deeper and deeper inside, making it harder to heal, at the same time. Your ability to show mercy is the sign that your character is growing strong; your feelings of resentment are the sign that your shame is thwarting that.

A number of things are good for your growth as a person; resentment is not one of them. Taking the focus off of the people you resent and unearthing your hidden feelings of shame that have been triggered by what they have done to you is the beginning point of healing. You can't do this all by yourself, but it can be done. I know because I have witnessed it many times when working with courageous people like Michael.

CHAPTER SEVEN

How to Heal
Envy and Jealousy

You were created for the purpose of having joyful relationships. That's why you are here. But the only way to have joyful relationships is to be emotionally vulnerable. This means you are inherently vulnerable and dependent on your relationships to be who you were created to be. I know this is hard for most people to accept, but being vulnerable and dependent is not a weakness; it is a fundamental characteristic of your ontology (the nature of being). I am not saying it feels good to be vulnerable and dependent on others; it is actually frightening most of the time. But that doesn't change the fact that this is how God made you to be if you want to find real joy in life.

Shame is the enemy of vulnerability. Shame is the painful reaction to anticipated or real rejection. It makes us want to hide—the opposite of vulnerability. Interestingly, the situation is not what causes us to feel shame, but our interpretation of it. Although there are a few circumstances in which almost everyone would feel shame, most situations turn out to produce shame in some people but not in others. When it comes to shame, a lot is in the eye of the beholder.

So if your interpretation of an event leads you to feel rejected (or to fear being rejected), you are likely to feel shame because of it. And you are not going to want to be vulnerable if this happens. Quite the opposite, you are going to be looking for some way to escape the pain you are now in.

If your purpose is to be vulnerable and dependent on your joyful relationships, and something makes you afraid that you are going to be rejected, the painful feeling of shame that follows is a pretty important reaction that demands some attention. You see, shame not only makes you want to hide, but it also makes you *self-focused*. Unlike guilt, which makes you focus on what you *did* that was wrong, shame makes you focus on *being* wrong. Shame makes you suspicious that the rejection you are feeling is not being caused by something you did; it is being caused by something you are. Now you have the feeling that something is very, very wrong; and you fear the problem is you. So you start to wonder things like, *Is this my fault?* or *Why does this keep happening?* or even *Is it me?*

You don't want to feel bad about yourself. That would be too violating to your deep longing to live in joyful relationships. Far down inside, you want to be accepted, so this horrible feeling of shame forces you to do something to protect yourself. Unfortunately, shame is a very bad motivator of good behavior. Because you feel bad about yourself, you are likely to make bad choices to try to fix the situation. And two of the most insidiously bad reactions to the painful feeling of shame are envy and jealousy. They rarely help the situation, but they are extremely popular reactions nonetheless.

Envy and Jealousy

Jealousy is the fear that something or someone important to you is about to be taken from you. It involves a three-way triangle that sets up a competition for love. Jealousy involves you, the person you love, and a rival. It is not necessarily pathological, but when it is intense and it goes on for very long, it certainly can be. Jealousy alerts you to the fact that something is wrong in a significant relationship and you need to pay attention or you are about to end up losing something very valuable. Sometimes jealousy also involves feelings of envy, but they are not the same thing.

Envy is the hatred you feel toward another person who reminds you of what you are not. This is a two-person dynamic between you and one other person. With envy, you see qualities in someone else that trigger feelings of shame in you. Looking at this other person makes you realize that they are the person *you* should be, but you know in your heart that you are not that person. It is as if they are rubbing it in your face; you have failed to be the person you know you were supposed to be. And there they are, dancing around right in front of you, being all perfect and great, making you feel bad about yourself. So what do you do? You hate them. With envy.

Both envy and jealousy are emotions of comparison. You are comparing yourself to someone else, and you fear you are coming up short. Both feelings are a threat to your sense of self, and both feelings are very dangerous to your joyful relationships with God and others. And as you have learned, both feelings are made much worse when they are being driven by shame-proneness. Nothing good comes out of the unconscious belief that you are worthless, defective, and inadequate. Once that gets established, things only get worse.

The Elephant and the Rider

From the publication of Charles Darwin's *The Expression of the Emotions in Man and Animals* in 1872 until now, scientists have been trying to understand the role of feelings in human behavior. Darwin saw emotions as the source of motivation, which is pretty much how contemporary psychologists view them today. *E-motions* are the quickest way we can assess what is happening, and they stimulate us toward movement. Psychologists used to think that the power of insight and rational thinking was the best way to make changes. Cleaning up our cognitive distortions was a very popular approach to helping people in past decades. Many psychologists don't think this is quite right anymore. Now we are recognizing the power that our emotions have to produce change, a much more powerful force than we previously appreciated.

A popular metaphor of a small rider on top of a large elephant is often used to explain the power of emotions.[1] Your rational thinking is like the small rider attempting to direct the mammoth beast underneath. Your emotions are like the giant elephant who can be controlled but who under certain circumstances may go stampeding off down any path if the motivation to move in that direction is strong enough. You may think you are in control of your feelings, but that is only if your feelings are willing to submit to the authority of your rational mind.

Because of all the advances in neuroscience, we now know that the emotional part of the brain is many times faster than the rational part of the brain. So in most situations, we are feeling something long before we know what we think about it. We draw emotional conclusions very quickly, and most of the choices we make are powerfully motivated by a "sense" we have about things, or a "gut reaction" that we don't fully understand. Every marketing executive, politician, or effective leader of any kind knows that people make most of their choices based on their feelings. Many times we make up a rational explanation for the decisions we make because we have already come to an emotional conclusion and we now just need something intelligent sounding to go along with it. We think we are basically rational persons, but the truth is, we are more rationalizing persons than we realize. The rider on the elephant is quite small by comparison. He can control the beast, but only if the beast allows it.

Envy, jealousy, and even shame all are emotions. They are the elephant we are trying to guide from our position as a tiny rider over them. Because these emotions strike at the core of our sense of self and threaten our created purpose to live in joyful relationships, they are very powerful and difficult to manage. Once they have triggered the unconscious process that leads to shame-proneness, we are very much in danger of the elephant charging off in whatever direction it likes, with our rational minds left to hold on for dear life. Reasoning with an extremely jealous person is very difficult, and it is even more useless to argue with someone in the midst of an envious rage.

WHAT ABOUT BOB?

Bob is an intelligent and ambitious businessman who got his break in the textile industry when Timothy, a friend of his father, offered to take him in and train him. Bob worked hard because he was grateful to have the opportunity to learn from one of the leaders in his business and because they were both Christians. Timothy was happy to teach him everything he knew to help him succeed. Although they never formally labeled their relationship, it was clear to both that Timothy was Bob's mentor, and both men felt the personal affection between them that good mentoring relationships can produce.

Both Timothy and Bob were successful for several years, and Timothy could not have been happier with their relationship. However, for Bob, things gradually changed. Unfortunately, Bob had a demanding and critical father who left him with deep scars about his sense of worth, especially when he was around men in positions of authority. Every success he achieved growing up was not quite good enough. And every time he looked to his father for praise, all he got was advice on how he could do better. This type of overfocus on performance by a father is damaging to a boy's sense of self, and it often leaves the child with doubts about his value. Although you would never know it by looking at him, Bob suffered from lifelong feelings of shame. He hid it well with all his success and achievements, but Bob was shame-prone down deep inside.

Sadly, many mentoring relationships end badly because the man receiving the mentoring has unresolved issues with his father. A good mentoring relationship is a powerful resource for anyone wanting to be successful. In fact, most successful businesspeople report that they owe their success in large part to their mentors. But because the mentoring relationship is personal, men receiving the mentoring often confuse their mentors with their fathers. Of course women do this too, but I think you can see how problematic it is for men who have male mentors when they have hidden feelings of shame that were planted there by the treatment they received from their fathers. Fathers are supposed to teach boys how to become men, but raising them with constant criticism is not a very good way to do that.

Fathers and mentors play two different roles in the life of a man. Fathers and sons have a love relationship with each other that they need to work out. Mentors and those they mentor are actually in love with their work, not each other. This can be confusing, and it certainly was for Bob. Timothy offered Bob support and direction to help him succeed in the business world that they both loved. But Bob couldn't help feeling that Timothy wasn't being honest with him. Sure, Timothy always said positive things about Bob to his face, but what was he really thinking that he wasn't saying? Bob was convinced that Timothy was secretly critical of him and that he didn't believe that Bob had what it took to be a success. Bob assumed that Timothy was thinking about him exactly as his father used to but that Timothy wasn't honest enough to say it out loud.

Bob couldn't help it. He was in the grips of the unconscious belief that when negative things happened, he should feel ashamed of himself. So when things didn't go right at work, Bob was convinced that Timothy blamed it on him—personally. Bob knew his performance was good, but he couldn't shake the feeling that he still felt bad about himself around Timothy and that Timothy must be to blame for it.

For the first several years of their relationship, Bob looked up to Timothy and almost idolized him. Timothy was the model of success, and Bob wanted to be just like him. But as time went on, Bob's idealization of Timothy changed from a source of comfort to a source of resentment. At first Bob felt good about his dependency on Timothy. How else was he going to learn everything he needed to know to be successful? But over time Bob grew to resent his dependency on Timothy, and instead of feeling glad he worked for such a well-known person in the industry, Bob hated feeling like he was always living in his shadow. Bob no longer respected Timothy for being successful; now he envied him for it. Now, instead of feeling good about working for Timothy, Bob felt bad. And envy is not a passive form of anger; it is malicious in that it makes the envious person want to destroy the person who makes them feel those painful feelings of shame.

You could say that Bob was jealous of Timothy, and that would be correct. Timothy was successful, knowledgeable, and certainly a worthy rival if you wanted to compete with him for success. But more importantly, Bob was envious of Timothy, and this made him grow in his hatred of him over the years. Every time Bob thought about Timothy's achievements, he wasn't inspired to want to do the same someday; instead, he felt bad about who he was today. And even though he couldn't admit it, Bob hated Timothy for that.

Jealousy makes you want to win something. Envy makes you want to spoil it. Although he never disclosed any of his feelings to Timothy, Bob started planning to damage Timothy's success so that he wouldn't feel so inadequate around him. He began having secret meetings with Timothy's key vendors, and he promised to make them more successful than they could ever be working with Timothy. Bob would focus on things Timothy did that he could criticize, and he developed personal relationships with several clients so that he could use his relationships with them to convince them to move their business from Timothy over to a new company that Bob had been forming. Bob kept assuring Timothy that everything was fine and that he was grateful for the training he received and loyal to Timothy because of it. He knew he was being deceitful, but he convinced himself that Timothy owed him everything he was taking for all his years of service. He knew this would hurt Timothy, but because envy limits a person's ability to have empathy, he just didn't care.

Sensing that something was wrong, Timothy invited Bob over to his house for dinner so they could sit down with their wives and discuss the future. The four of them had known one another for years, so Bob and his wife had been to Timothy's home many times. Timothy knew that Bob was restless and that it might be time for him to strike out on his own. He truly wanted the best for Bob, so if they were going to part ways, Timothy wanted them to do it well.

At one point in the evening, Timothy turned to Bob and said, "Just let me know what you want to do, Bob. And that is what we will make happen."

Bob's wife jumped in. "Go ahead, tell him. Timothy loves you.

Just tell him what's in your heart." She was fully aware of all the clandestine meetings Bob had been having with Timothy's clients, and she wanted her husband to step up and be honest about his plans. They were all Christians, so there shouldn't be any need to do things in secret.

"I don't know," Bob mumbled. "I'm just not sure."

"Whatever you want, I want to help you achieve it," Timothy said.

"I hear those words," Bob replied, "but I just can't believe them."

Bob was in the grips of his deepest envy and shame. His unresolved rage toward his father for all those years of belittling him was now focused on Timothy, and he couldn't surrender it. Bob never felt that his own father believed in him, so how could he possibly think that Timothy could? Bob couldn't admit that he felt inferior around Timothy, because this was a deeply held unconscious belief triggered by his feelings of envy and shame. No one is aware of being in the grips of unconscious beliefs, because they happen outside of one's awareness. A person isn't aware that they are believing they are worthless, they just simply feel that it is true. Bob knew he felt bad around Timothy, but he needed to blame Timothy for it. Confessing that he felt worthless would have been too vulnerable. Blaming Timothy for how bad he felt gave him a reason outside of himself to explain his pain. That was certainly preferable to looking inside himself and opening up the feelings of self-doubt and insecurity that were the real source of his envy.

Shame-proneness causes people to blame others. Shame is a horrible feeling, and the chronic nature of shame-proneness is exhausting. To survive it, blame is a handy tool to find some relief. If someone else is to blame for how bad you feel, you get a temporary reprieve from feeling bad about yourself. And when shame-proneness causes you to feel envy, you not only want to blame someone, but now you want to damage that person as well.

Later that week Bob announced his plan to start a company of his own. He took two key people from Timothy's company and formed a new one where Bob could be the top person. In their first staff meeting, Bob strongly proclaimed that they were going to be the best company in the textile industry. At one point his feelings got the better of him and he slammed his fist down on the table, angrily insisting that they were going to "crush" Timothy and his company. *He* was the leader of the industry now, and everyone was going to recognize it.

Of course the relationship between Bob and Timothy was severed. This was one of those mentoring relationships that did not end well. Timothy wanted to talk with Bob about what happened, but they could never have an honest conversation about it. Bob thought it was just business. Timothy knew it was deeply personal. But talking about shame and envy is extremely difficult. Shame makes us want to hide, not reconcile. Shame makes us want to blame, not be vulnerable. And envy makes us want to use anger to spoil others in destructive ways, not solve problems between people. Unless Bob was willing to have the courage to face his shame and acknowledge the destructive envy he felt toward Timothy, he was never going to repair their relationship. And sadly, this was just not something he was ever able to do.

You might think that Bob was not really a Christian. I mean, he was dishonest and prideful, and he certainly did not conduct himself in a loving manner. But I don't think this is right. I have worked with many Christians over the years who have been so blinded by their shame and envy that they couldn't listen to what the Bible, other believers, or even the Holy Spirit was saying to them. I have seen church leaders fire pastors out of envy, pastors destroy the reputations of other pastors out of envy, and basically good people do very bad things because of it as well. Envy is a very destructive emotion, and because it focuses on someone else, it can convince you that the anger you feel is justified, or even righteous. Bob convinced himself that what happened between him and Timothy was actually just a disagreement regarding matters of opinion. He never could admit to himself that what he did was motivated by destructive feelings of envy and shame.

Shame leads to all kinds of psychological problems, and when it leads to envy, it is particularly dangerous because of its destructive nature. Because shame makes us want to hide, we often don't even know that we are feeling it when we are envious. All we know is that the other person needs to be stopped, taken down a notch, or taught a lesson. Because of Bob's envy, he felt justified in destroying the most significant mentoring relationship he had ever had. The elephant underneath him was too powerful to be stopped by any advice, reasoning, or even the pleas of his own wife. Recognizing envy when you see it in other people is very important, but recognizing it when you are feeling it yourself is even more important.

IDEALIZATION

Idealization is a good thing. For the first several years of their relationship, Bob's idealization of Timothy motivated him to grow and become a better man. When people are feeling true idealization, they feel comforted in the presence of the respected authority they idealize. We were created to seek out an ideal God and find comfort in our relationship with him. We have that same comfort, along with security, in our human relationships when we find parents, teachers, and mentors we can idealize. As we grow in these human relationships, that idealization turns into a mutual respect. As mature adults we worship an ideal God, and we respect wise men and women who inspire us toward growth. This is all good.

But some idealization is not as it appears to be. Sometimes we actually *idolize* others in ways that are not good for us, or even for them. In these instances we are not motivated to grow and become better people, and we don't really feel secure because of the person we are idolizing, because we are actually using our idolizing as a way of covering over our insecurity. As Bob's shame-proneness surfaced in his relationship with Timothy, he was no longer comforted by Timothy's greater experience and knowledge. Then Bob started to feel inferior to Timothy, and he had to compensate for his feelings of inferiority. At this point he would make comments about Timothy's accomplishments, but instead of being inspired, now Bob was envious, so he became mocking and sarcastic instead of genuinely complimentary of Timothy.

Idealization can be very confusing. Perhaps you have witnessed someone who appeared to be idealizing someone else, but the tone of the comments being made were actually not positive. They might say things like, "Oh, sure he is very successful. But what did he have to do to get there?" or "She is really pretty, but I think it goes to her head"; or "He's the smartest guy I know, but he thinks he's the smartest guy *he* knows too."

These are certainly positive traits being talked about, but the comments being made are not positive. This is not true idealization in the way the God created it to be. These are actually instances of envy. What the person is doing is describing a quality they wish was true of themselves that they see in someone else, but they don't really feel this quality is true of them. That's envy. They have an ideal for themselves that they wish was true, but it isn't, so they are defensively mocking that quality when they see it in someone else.

Idealizing someone we respect is a developmental process, which means the feelings develop and grow as we do. We idealize them until we grow to respect them. This is a good thing, and it is how God created us to be. We are looking for a perfect God to idealize, and we look to other people in our lives to look up to for comfort and guidance along the way. We never lose our need to seek out an ideal God. We don't outgrow that need, but we will move from idealization of others to a more mature form of respect for them as we grow.

Defensively idolizing someone does not lead to growth. It is a substitution for the natural developmental process with a defensive idolization of others to cover over insecurities and shame. You see greatness around you, but it doesn't inspire you to grow toward it. It only makes you envious, which motivates you to spoil what you see in others that you only wish you could see in yourself. So if there is someone in your life you look up to with respect, or perhaps even idealize, that is probably a good thing. If you envy that person, well, that simply is not a good thing.

SCARCITY OR PLENTY?

There are two basic attitudes you can have about the world around you and the resources in it: *scarcity* and *plenty*. All too often an attitude of scarcity is fueled by shame and comparison. If you feel that you are not enough, you will feel that there never is enough—of anything. Scarcity is a way of attributing this feeling of not enough to the external world around you rather than locating the origin of that feeling within yourself. Would you rather feel that you are not enough or that you are just not getting enough? I think we all know the answer to that.

If our basic need is for joyful relationships with God and others, we are fundamentally created for connection. But an attitude of scarcity replaces connection with competition, and not in a good way.

Not all competition is bad. When you compete with others to do your best, you may be inspired to grow and mature your abilities. When this is your motivation, you view your competitors with respect and with the attitude that there is plenty of talent and ability to go around. But when you compete with others to see them defeated, you may be driven by an attitude of scarcity. Now you view your competitors as enemies, and you are more driven by the fear of defeat than the love of success. An attitude of scarcity fuels envy and jealousy because scarcity is the enemy of connection and belonging, and it is based on the notion that you must defeat competitors to survive. Scarcity causes you to feel that losing means *you* are a loser, because the attitude of scarcity is motivated by shame.

An attitude of scarcity is often a spiritual problem. If it is rooted in the belief that you are not enough, it will cause you to compete with others for what you believe are limited resources for your survival. But to thrive in life, you must see others as a needed resource for your survival, not a threat to it. This comes through the spiritual attitude of plenty.

Jesus said, "Are not two sparrows sold for a penny? Yet not one of them will fall to the ground outside your Father's care. And even the very hairs of your head are all numbered. So don't be afraid; you are worth more than many sparrows" (Matthew 10:29-31). He was pointing us to an attitude of plenty, the opposite of scarcity. Yes, we have to work hard to eat well, and we should take care of our physical bodies (all of which the Bible addresses elsewhere), but what attitude should we have as we are doing so? Jesus is not saying you should be lazy and not care about the physical things of life; he is talking about your attitude. An attitude of scarcity will cause you to envy others and see them as your adversaries for limited resources, which means that when they win you lose. As their value increases, your value decreases. But grasping the fact that you are small in the physical universe but still have ultimate value because of your relationship with God frees you from an attitude of scarcity. An attitude of plenty empowers you to be vulnerable with others and open to a connection with them, not blinded by your view of them as competitors to be defeated. Now losing can have multiple meanings, and not one of them is that you are worthless. You will have ups and downs in life, but your value will not be the least bit diminished because of them. This is an attitude of plenty.

Is Envy or Jealousy Ever a Good Thing?

Jealousy is not always a bad thing. God even refers to himself as a "jealous God" at times (for example, Exodus 20:5). This obviously means there are times to be jealous and protective of something or someone you love. It is hard to imagine any seriously romantic relationship where the partners would not want to protect the intimate nature of their relationship from would-be rivals seeking to break it up. If you never felt jealousy of any kind in a romantic relationship, your partner might well question whether you were truly in love. At the very least, feelings of jealousy can alert you that something might be in need of your attention. Your jealousy might be telling you to listen better, express your affection more often, or simply pay more attention to the one you love. In all these ways, jealousy can be a good thing.

But I don't have to tell you that jealousy can also be a bad thing. Marriages have ended because of it, wars have been fought, mental patients have been diagnosed with a delusional form of it, and we even have special laws governing crimes of passion, which signifies that the judicial system recognizes the distorting power jealousy can have on human judgment.[2] So what's the difference between good jealousy and the bad kind? Shame. Underlying every destructive expression of jealousy you will find intense, long-standing feelings of shame. People who are prone to shame have a difficult time managing all of their emotions, and jealousy is no exception. Once shame gets involved, you are no longer just trying to protect someone or something you love; now you are aggressively fighting to keep from being exposed as a loser, or someone who is not worthy of love.

So idealization can be a good thing, but envy is not. Likewise, jealousy used to protect love can be a good thing, but jealousy laced with shame is not. I think you can see the pattern here. Momentary feelings can alert us to issues in our relationships and help us maintain joyful connections to God and others. But chronic feelings of shame will eventually confirm beliefs within us that we are worthless, and this never leads to anything good. In other words, if you are having a problem with envy or jealousy, you are actually having a problem with shame. And if your problems in these areas have gone on for very long at all, you are becoming shame-prone, and this is something you are going to need to address.

CHAPTER EIGHT

The Secret Cause
of Narcissism

So what is a chapter on narcissism doing in a book on shame? Most people think of narcissists as people who love themselves too much, have too much self-esteem, and conduct themselves in a shameless manner most of the time. A common notion is that narcissistic people should be ashamed of themselves more often, rather than thinking they have an excess of shame.

Although not obvious on the surface most of the time, there is a definite relationship between narcissism and shame. Psychologists have been studying this very carefully, and they have come up with some important findings that you would do well to be aware of. If you think you might have a narcissistic person in your life, you are going to want to read this chapter.

WHAT IS NARCISSISM?

The word *narcissism* comes from the Greek myth of Narcissus, who was an extremely handsome hunter known for his physical beauty. The nymph Echo fell in love with Narcissus, but he rejected her, causing her to disappear into the woods until all that was left was her echo. Nemesis, the goddess of revenge, then led Narcissus to a pool of water where he fell in love with his own image. When he finally recognized that his love could never be reciprocated, Narcissus committed suicide. His grandiose opinion of his own attractiveness and exaggerated self-focus led to the modern use of the word *narcissism*.

The term was first used by psychologists in 1898, and then it was introduced into the *Diagnostic and Statistical Manual* (DSM), which all psychologists use to diagnose mental problems, in 1980 under the heading of Narcissistic Personality Disorder (NPD). Because of the controversy over labeling people with personality disorders, psychologists almost took NPD out of the latest version of the DSM but then decided to leave in it. The way we think about it now is that all people are narcissistic to some degree, but there are some people who have a pathological degree of narcissism that we all need to recognize.

In short, someone who is predisposed to excessive narcissism lacks empathy and has problems with intimacy. Their relationships tend to be superficial, and they are prone to grandiosity and attention-seeking behavior. Their exaggerated opinion of themselves can flip between the extremes of believing they are the best at everything to being convinced they are the worst, but they characteristically gravitate to the furthest end of whatever continuum they are applying to themselves. Most psychologists distinguish between narcissism as a trait and NPD as a personality disorder because, as I said, we all are narcissistic to some degree. In other words, we all are self-focused and need attention from time to time.

Some people get NPD confused with the more extreme Antisocial Personality Disorder, which is much worse. People with this particular set of problems are manipulative, deceitful, callous, and hostile. They are irresponsible and impulsive, and they take risks at others' expense. The old terms for these people are *sociopaths* and *psychopaths*, and these are the really bad people among us. I am going to say a bit more about them later, but Antisocial Personality Disorder is much less common than NPD and much more dangerous.

ARE THERE TWO KINDS OF NARCISSISM?

Unfortunately, experts can't agree on the exact cause of narcissism or on all of its manifestations. Clinicians (the psychologists who actually treat people in therapy) are very convinced that shame is the underlying cause of narcissism, but researchers (the psychologists that conduct scientific studies in laboratories) are having a hard time proving this with their research.[1] If you think about it, this makes sense. What narcissistic person is going to want to answer questions honestly in a study on narcissism if that study has even a chance of making that person look bad? Especially if shame is really the underlying cause of narcissism, studying it is going to be difficult. One way psychologists like to get around this is by trying to divide narcissism into two different types. That way, if we disagree, we don't have to determine who is wrong; we can just say we are talking about two different things.

Some psychologists think there are two extreme types of narcissism: grandiosity and inferiority. Others think there is a healthy narcissism and then an unhealthy type that goes to extremes. I don't think there actually are two kinds of narcissism, but narcissism is something that makes people want to go to the extreme to get others' attention.

We all want others to think well of us. You were created for joyful relationships, so how you conduct yourself around others matters. Adopting the position that you don't care about what other people think is not a sign of health. This callousness is not a natural part of how you were made to be. You just don't want to go to the extreme of letting popular opinion determine your choices.

Jesus was getting at this idea when he said, "Woe to you when everyone speaks well of you" (Luke 6:26). He was basically telling us not to make our choices based on the approval of others, because this extreme attention-seeking behavior is too narcissistic (okay, he didn't use that term, but I think he would have if he had it). But on the other hand, the apostle John had no problem saying of his friend, "Demetrius is well spoken of by everyone" (3 John 1:12), because a person's reputation as an upstanding and moral person is always a good thing. So even though technically caring about what other people think of you is narcissistic, that is not a problem as long as it does not go to an extreme.

The same thing can be said for feelings of inferiority. As I pointed our earlier, at times you need to recognize that you are less than others. While this is sometimes painful, it is also sometimes a helpful form of humility. But God does not want you to take this to the extreme of self-loathing. We are instructed, "In humility value others above yourselves" (Philippians 2:3), but we are also reminded that we are made just "a little lower than the angels" (Hebrews 2:7). Extreme self-hatred is a form of what psychologists call *negative narcissism*, and this is not what God has in mind for you. You are not the best, but you are certainly not the worst either. Thinking that you are is really just a form of narcissistic grandiosity.

When you boil it down, the essence of narcissism is just the yearning to be unique or special to others.[2] God made you with this yearning, so this is a good thing. When this need is met with a positive response, all goes well for you. When it is ignored or rejected, the result is shame. When shame enters the picture, everything changes. What we might call *normal narcissistic* needs change into something different. Now you don't simply want to know that you are special because God created you to live in joyfully special relationships. No, now you want to have others *confirm* your specialness because you are starting to doubt it. Instead of being driven out of your God-instilled need for connection, now you are driven by your shame. And shame is rarely a good motivation for anything.

So there aren't two kinds of narcissism; there are just different motivations for it depending on the circumstances and the extremes to which people take it. The important thing here is that what does change narcissism is whether or not it is motivated by shame. The reasons clinicians are convinced that shame is the underlying cause of narcissism is that in psychotherapy we are mostly concerned about pathological extremes of narcissism, or what has been labeled NPD. When narcissism becomes a problem, shame is always involved. Shame turns the need for connection into the need for attention, grandiosity, and a lack of empathy. Shame turns everyone's narcissism into extreme attention-getting behavior that turns out to be a problem.

So the extreme form of narcissism is the result of chronic feelings of shame. This shame-prone narcissism is what clinicians see in our offices all the time. Narcissism without shame just doesn't cause many problems, so we don't need to focus our attention on it. But narcissists who lack empathy, have exaggerated opinions of themselves and superficial relationships, and are prone to grandiosity and attention-seeking behavior are suffering from chronic feelings of shame. While we all have a narcissistic need to be thought well of by others, this transforms into a form of narcissism that can be damaging to our relationships when it is motivated by hidden feelings of shame.

ARROGANCE VERSUS CONFIDENCE

The main trick of narcissism is to make everyone think that everything is just fine. If everything is truly fine, your need for the approval from God and others is just a normal feeling of wanting good relationships to, in fact, be good. But if everything is *not* fine, such as when you have secret feelings of worthlessness or inferiority that you don't want anyone to know about, your narcissism is actually a disguise for how bad you feel about yourself.

This is seen pretty clearly in the difference between confidence and arrogance. Confidence is a good thing. You want to be confident in your relationship with God, confident in your God-given abilities, and confident in what you know to be true. But arrogance is shame disguised as confidence to distract others away from painful feelings you are hiding. A truly confident person is free to be humble, vulnerable, and transparent because that person has nothing to hide. But an arrogant person only *appears* to be confident; the true motivation for their behavior is to avoid exposing their shame.

Think back to when you were in high school. Remember the mean girls or stuck-up guys? On the surface they acted like everyone wanted to be just like them. They were exclusive, demeaning, and self-focused, and they had an exaggerated view of their own attractiveness. In short, they were driven by shame-prone narcissism. Even though they always wanted to be at the "see and be seen" parties, the truth is they were fighting off painful feelings of insecurity that they didn't want anyone to see at all. That form of narcissism is exploitative of others and based on feelings of entitlement that keep relationships superficial and far away from any vulnerability that would expose their hidden shame. Even though they acted like it, they actually were not confident at all—they were arrogant.

When you are around someone who is arrogant, you don't feel very good. You don't want to be vulnerable because you don't sense any vulnerability in them. They may be very extroverted and even self-disclosing, but you don't really feel connected to them. Arrogant people want you to feel good about *them*, confident people are okay with you feeling good about *you*. This is a pretty big difference.

Have you ever wondered if you were confusing confidence and arrogance? It's not hard to do. Some theologians think the apostle Paul was sorting this out by using his own life as an example in passages like 2 Corinthians 11:16–12:10 where he "boasts" in his suffering for Christ. Because of what was going on in Corinth, he felt forced to make the point that if others could boast about their worldly accomplishments, he could certainly do the same, but the only thing worth boasting about was how God's power is made more evident through our weaknesses. Even though Paul may have been tempted to boast at times, he was committed to the belief that all that matters is our relationships with God, and drawing attention to ourselves for any other reason is just narcissistic (again, my term, not his).

Sometimes we are accidentally arrogant when we are trying to be confident because we don't see the feelings of shame driving us. We want to convince others of the correctness of our position, but we make them uncomfortable with our lack of humility in the way we are saying it. It is in those moments that we are being influenced by our shame rather than confidence. We may say things like, "Well, I think they were just being *convicted* because they knew what I was saying was true," when there may have been something else going on (like you were embarrassing them). True confidence draws others toward us; arrogance will drive them away.

As always, Jesus is the perfect example. You can pick any one of the examples of Jesus conversing with people in the Bible and come away with the same conclusion. He was completely confident, certain of what he was saying, and humble enough to make whomever he was talking to feel intimately special and known. He didn't need to boast so that they would know that he was special; he focused on them so they could feel special themselves. Take the example of the Samaritan woman at the well (John 4). It was politically incorrect for him even to be talking to a woman of her low social class, but after only a few minutes of conversation, she felt so listened to, so understood, so intimately known that she ran back to her town and told everyone, "Come, see a man who told me everything I ever did" (verse 29). Her larger-than-life report of what happened between her and Jesus lets us know that she had just been in the presence of divine confidence, and she knew it.

SHAME AND ANGER

Some anger is a good thing, and some is not. Anger is an emotion created by God to motivate us to take care of problems. Remember that Paul said, "'In your anger do not sin': Do not let the sun go down while you are still angry" (Ephesians 4:26). Like most emotions, anger is meant to be experienced as a short-term feeling and not intended to be something that goes on for a long time. When it does, you probably have not solved the problem for which it was intended. This, of course, will produce other problems.

Not surprisingly, anger and shame don't mix well. Unlike guilt, which is the bad feeling you get for having done something wrong, shame is the bad feeling that you *are* something wrong, so when you get angry you are very likely to misuse your anger. Paul's warning that you can easily sin when you are angry is especially true when you are feeling shame at the same time. Shame motivates you to hide, distract others away from focusing attention on your flaws, and direct your anger outward. This makes using the energy of your anger to solve problems constructively very difficult.

People who are prone to responding with shame have particularly maladaptive responses to anger. They often hurt others without thinking through the consequences of their behavior. When they get mad, they want to quickly attribute their failings to external causes or other people, which makes problem solving more difficult. Anger makes you want to focus your attention on a problem; shame makes you want to focus your anger on a person. So the next time you get mad at someone, you need to ask yourself a question. Are you mad at that person because that person is really the problem, or are you mad at them because of your own shame? Anger is your God-given energy to solve a problem; shame makes you want to direct your anger at someone else and make that person the problem instead.

NARCISSISTIC RAGE

Let's kick it up a notch. There is anger, and then there is *rage*— a more intense form of anger that is volatile and dangerous. People can be motivated to become rageful for various reasons, and one of them is what psychologists call *narcissistic rage*.

If narcissism is a problem when it is driven by shame, then anger that is driven by shame is an even greater problem. Narcissistic rage is the furious anger that explodes when shame-prone narcissism is punctured or thwarted. Narcissism that is motivated by shame is fragile and renders a person susceptible to psychological injury. The typical narcissistic exaggerated focus on self-importance, grandiosity, and attention-seeking behavior can appear to be coming from someone who is confident and strong, but as I just mentioned, this form of shame-prone narcissism is actually displaying arrogance that is a disguise for underlying shame. If you confront, expose, or embarrass someone who is in the midst of being arrogant, you run the risk of narcissistically injuring this person. Their arrogance is only a cover-up for painful feelings they are trying to hide. If you expose those feelings, often what you get is narcissistic rage.

Narcissistic rage is a defense against shame. For the narcissisti-cally injured person, the best defense is a good offense. Sometimes a person in the midst of a narcissistic rage can even dissociate, or lose conscious awareness of what they are doing. They may remember what you said that made them so mad, but they may not actually remember what they did when they were in their rage.

This form of rage is what psychologists call an *antidote* to power-lessness. This means the narcissistically injured person feels humili-ated and powerless, but their rage gives them the illusion that they are powerful and back in control. They are typically actually out of control, and able to do and say things they may later regret deeply, but when they are in the middle of a narcissistic rage, they feel strong, invulnerable, and powerful. We call this an antidote because it is not actually a cure for powerlessness but only a temporary form of self-medication. What would you rather feel, shame and powerlessness, or rage? People with shame-prone narcissism almost always choose rage.

You may know someone with this problem. You probably have said they had a problem with anger or anger management. Now you know this person has problem with shame. I know a business con-sultant who works with managers referred to him for anger issues. He has noticed an interesting thing: Every one of those managers sent to him to work on their anger management issues reported the same thing—they never once blew up at a superior; they only went into rages on their subordinates. They could manage their anger when they had to, but what they couldn't manage was their narcis-sistically injured shame.

Justin's Story

Justin had a difficult childhood. He grew up in an African-American family where his father struggled to provide for them, so his father was not around very much, and when he was, he was tired and irritable. His mother was overwhelmed by life and usually just didn't want to be bothered by Justin, so he remembers growing up with her locked in her bedroom most of the day, leaving him and his siblings to fend for themselves. If he tried to bring up anything to his parents, he would receive criticism for bothering them. Justin grew up feeling very disconnected from pretty much everyone, which means he felt lonely and worthless most of the time.

Fortunately, Justin is very intelligent, and this goes a long way in terms of helping a young black man survive in the world. He didn't have many friends, and his study habits were bad given his difficult home environment, but his natural intelligence was enough for Justin to make it all the way through college and earn his degree— a pretty significant accomplishment for someone with his background. After college Justin started his own consulting firm and made a decent living in the area of technology. He built the company up to where he had several employees. This success was so helpful for Justin's self-esteem that he was able to get married and have a couple of kids of his own. Despite his humble beginnings and the racial cards that were stacked against him, Justin had made a success of himself, and for that he was quite proud.

But none of us get to escape difficult childhoods without some scars. Justin was educated and successful and had an attractive wife and family to prove how well he was doing in life. But the effect of growing up with years of feeling lonely, worthless, and discriminated against do not just go away. Justin doesn't like to admit it, but he still struggles with deep feelings of self-doubt today. He kept his struggles to himself, trying to white-knuckle his way through life, but this strategy just wasn't making the feelings leave.

Justin ended up in my office when his wife demanded that he get help for his anger problem. He had been having explosive fits of anger for years, and she couldn't deal with them anymore. His anger was wearing her down and damaging the children. She said she loved him, but either he had to go to therapy or she was going to leave him. He had to figure himself out or get out—the choice was his. Justin chose therapy.

As he sat across from me, Justin looked down at the floor and said, "I hate myself for all the things I have done over the years."

"You mean the things you did when you were angry?" I asked.

"I don't just get mad," Justin replied. "I lose it. You don't know; you've never seen me when I get that way. It's like I'm a different person. I could do anything to anyone when I get that angry. It's pretty scary."

"So, you hate yourself for getting that angry?" I said.

"Right," Justin mumbled.

"I think you get that angry because you hate yourself," I said.

"What?" Justin seemed surprised.

"You think you feel guilty for what you have done to the people you love," I said.

"Shouldn't I?" Justin asked with irritation in his voice.

"Oh, I think it is much worse than that," I said.

"What do you mean?" he asked.

"I don't think you just feel guilt for what you've done. I think the reason you get so angry is that you feel ashamed of who you are. Your problems run much deeper than guilt, and you and I have some work to do to get to the bottom of it," I said.

Justin had overcome some challenging things in life. And he should feel proud of himself for doing so. But there is a difference between *feeling* proud and *being* proud. Feeling proud is when you have accomplished things that make others respect you, and that respect makes them want to connect with you. We feel pride when we have acted in ways our community admires, so we are respected and valued by others. This is a good thing. But being proud is a defense shame, the kind of pride the Bible says is toxic. Being proud is when you shut out other people and have an exaggerated view of your own opinion. This is shame-prone narcissism, and it disconnects you from others. This is not a good thing, and Justin was going to have to figure this out.

Justin had to get educated, overcome racial prejudice, build a successful business, and then learn to be intimate with his wife and family. And he had to do this all by himself. His father was too critical and his mother was too depressed, and society looked down on him as a second-class citizen. The chronic shame of his childhood had resulted in a narcissistic personality that served him well when it came to the ambition that he needed to be a success at school or in his business. But this shame-prone narcissism was not serving him well at home. Justin's wife was too educated, and the church they attended was too sophisticated to allow Justin's anger to go unnoticed. They knew his rages were an indication that something was wrong, and simply dismissing them as an "issue with anger" was not the loving thing to do. They were going to hold him accountable to be the loving man that they knew he wanted to be. And there was no way that was going to happen unless Justin was willing to deal honestly with his shame.

Justin was going to have to do everything he didn't want to do to deal with his narcissistic rages. He was going to have to be vulnerable, talk about his feelings, and relive his past with me. He hated the very thought of doing any one of those things, but doing all three of them was exactly what we set out to do. I have worked with a lot of men like Justin, and they all have one thing in common that helps: They are hard workers. Justin fought with me, insisted that I could never understand what it was like growing up as a black man, and used all the narcissistic defense mechanisms in the book. But he never gave up. He was no stranger to hard work, and our therapy together benefited from it.

Several months have passed since Justin has had an uncontrollable rage. I know, because some of them were with me in my office. That's why psychologists soundproof our office walls. We don't want to scare the neighbors. Therapy works because we enter into the vulnerable areas of life to bring healing there. But it is also in these vulnerable areas where people can get hurt. There were times when Justin was being vulnerable with me about very painful feelings of worthlessness, and even when I tried my best to be careful, he still would sometimes get narcissistically injured. This is part of the process. You can't perform surgery without causing pain and seeing your patient lose some blood. But each time that happened, Justin and I would do the hard work of repairing our relationship and the injury I had caused him during those vulnerable times.

Through this process of vulnerability and repairing the hurts that came from it, Justin and I were healing the wounds from his lonely childhood. He was not alone anymore. His feelings, especially the most private ones, were important. And when he felt this with me, an amazing thing started to happen. As he began to sense that his deepest feelings were valued, he also felt that *he* mattered too. If his vulnerable feelings had worth, maybe he did too.

Shame-prone narcissism is a problem, and narcissistic rage is one of the clearest symptoms of it. Although we like to think of narcissism as a discrete category of pathology, it is actually a relational event. The narcissistic yearning to be significant is present within all of us, but when we start to treat others like objects that exist only to get our own needs for attention met, we know that shame has taken over and we are no longer being driven by our need for joyful relationships. We all are narcissistic to some degree, but when our narcissism is motivated by shame, we only push others out of the way so we can focus all attention onto ourselves. And that doesn't result in joyful relationships at all.

NARCISSISM AND CRIMINAL BEHAVIOR

Criminals are selfish. They will take your things, take your time, and even take your life if they want it. This is shame-driven narcissism at its worst. The most extreme examples of this are sociopathy and psychopathy—when a person is willing to commit crimes without guilt or shame. Sociopathy and psychopathy are rare, and we don't know exactly what causes them, but there are people who lack a conscience and don't feel bad about themselves or what they have done. These people need to be kept separate from society because medical science doesn't yet have a cure for them. Of course, God can heal anything, and when he does heal something without a scientific cure, we call it a miracle because miracles don't depend on medical science.

Thankfully, most people who end up in jails and prisons are not sociopaths or psychopaths. They are mostly suffering from shame-prone narcissism. I bring this up because we all need to think long and hard about how to address bad behavior, both inside and outside of our criminal justice system. Some people think we need to confront narcissistic behavior and punish it to prevent it from happening again. I think our criminal justice system has proven quite convincingly that this doesn't work. The recidivism rate alone tells you that punishing people for acting badly does not inhibit future bad behavior. In other words, shaming people for shame-prone narcissism only makes things worse.

We know that guilt inhibits people from acting badly.[3] Shame doesn't. Shaming people to get them to improve their future moral behavior is wrongheaded. Shame doesn't make us want to be good;

love does. Dr. Byron Johnson is a criminologist who has spent his entire career studying the relationship between spirituality and crime, and he has concluded that we have today the most effective delivery system on the planet for the prevention of crime in even the most crime-ridden areas of society.[4] Do you know what that delivery system is? The Christian church.

That's right. The research is very convincing. The loving community of the Christian church does more to prevent crime, cut recidivism from prison, reduce drug use, lessen risky sexual behavior, decrease alcoholism, and help kids stay in school, get better grades, and find meaning and purpose in life than any other institution. Shaming people with shame-prone narcissism doesn't help them get better. Introducing them to the power of the Christian community does. I just thought you might like to know.

CHAPTER NINE

The Different Faces of Shame

Psychological problems always involve not being able to get along with other people. So you can't talk about mental issues without talking about relationships. If you have good relationships with others, you are probably mentally healthy. If you don't, well then you probably aren't. For your own mental health, it's important to understand the role that shame plays in your ability to have good relationships.

Because we all have feelings of shame, shame can manifest itself in about as many ways as there are people on the planet. Typically we think of people struggling with shame as having poor eye contact and slumped posture, and being withdrawn and too insecure to do much of anything. While this can be true, shame can also be the underlying motivation for a wide variety of things that may surprise you.

Shame causes us to disengage from our relationships with others. We fear rejection and have concern that we are unlovable and don't belong. These feelings cause us to react in extreme ways. We may try to be a perfectionist or resign ourselves to being a slob.

We may withdraw into depression or insist on being the center of attention. We may strive to be superspiritual or attempt suicide out of self-loathing. We may do everything for everyone to be a people pleaser, or we may act with complete disregard for the feelings of others to pursue our addictions. These are just a few of the ways shame can show up in our lives, but the point is that shame is associated with psychological problems that hurt our relationships with others. Let's take a look at a few of those problems.

PERFECTIONISM

One of the psychological problems that most often falls through the cracks during childhood is perfectionism. The reason is obvious: Perfectionists don't cause as many problems for others as they cause for themselves, so parents and teachers don't even think of perfectionism as a problem. Perfectionism is one of those manifestations of shame that you wouldn't suspect, at least not until you looked closely.

Take, for instance, the ten-year-old girl who spends several hours more than the other children to complete her homework, always feels compelled to do the extra credit, and changes her outfit several times a day to make sure it is right. Adults, seeing only her superficial practices, think she has the makings of the next president. But if they pay attention, they will notice some tension in her relationships with her peers, for she tends to be bossy and unforgiving. Moreover, the most telling sign of shame is that despite all the time and energy she puts into her perfectionism, it doesn't make her happy. She doesn't feel good when she gets all As; she just feels relieved that she didn't get an A-minus. The motivation for perfectionism is not the love of getting everything right; it is the fear of getting one thing wrong.

I know of one perfectionist girl who had to keep her room

completely organized or she would feel too anxious to go to sleep at night. All her stuffed animals had to be arranged in a row and all her clothes put away. Her closet had to be organized by color and function. She even went to the dry cleaners to ask for additional plastic covers so each hanger in her closet could have its own individual plastic cover separating it from the item next to it. Everything had its place, and everything had to be in it for her to feel okay.

But perfectionists never really feel okay. They are too concerned about something that happened in the past that wasn't right, or something that is going to happen in the future that might turn out wrong. The extraordinary effort that perfectionists put out to do life causes them to miss the joy in it because joy doesn't come from extraordinary effort; it comes from the ordinary moments available to all of us. We were designed by God to find joy in our simple relationships with him and others, not through special efforts to chase perfection.

Ironically, perfectionism is not the key to self-improvement or success. It can actually get in the way of it. If you are a perfectionist, you will spend too much time on things that are not really important, and you won't be able to prioritize the things that are necessary to work effectively. And most importantly, perfectionism does not avoid shame. It entrenches it. Perfectionism is the attempt to hide your fear that you are not enough (or too much) by getting everything just right. If you are good at it, you will only succeed at covering over your fear, never dispelling it. As soon as you have completed whatever it is that you are doing, you have to start over again immediately trying to do things perfectly to avoid your shame. You can never rest, because your strategy for hiding your shame can never heal it. Perfectionism isn't designed to do that; it is only designed to cover it over, leaving it painfully right where it always was—hidden inside of you.

There is nothing wrong with taking pride in a job well done. That is a sign of good mental health. To some degree you should care about what other people think. But perfectionism causes you to value what other people think to the exclusion of what you feel. When this happens you can't tell if something is good enough by simply looking at it; now you are terrorized by the fear of what other people might think about it. Shame hurts your ability to listen to yourself and God. It causes you to substitute the voices of other people in your head for what should be the ability to determine if something is good enough based on what you feel God wants of you.

If you are a perfectionist, I don't have to tell you that perfectionism leads to procrastination.[1] Starting and completing things can be difficult for a perfectionist. The anxiety of not getting something right makes the effort required to complete tasks more challenging than it needs to be. Shame-proneness will make you overly concerned with what other people are going to think about whatever it is you are doing, so simply following your own creativity becomes scary. What if you miss something or you don't think of everything? Putting off the finished product is a way of shielding yourself from the shame you are going to feel if something is not just right. If you are shame-prone, you won't just feel guilty for missing something; you will feel ashamed for being *the kind of person* who misses something. So the real reason you procrastinate is not that you just like to get things right; it's because you don't want an imperfection to expose your shame.

WITHDRAWAL

Withdrawal is the more familiar manifestation of shame. The feeling of shame causes us to disengage from others, making vulnerability more difficult, so wanting to hide is a common response to shame. When shame causes you to withdraw, you are likely to feel small or powerless and to have the desire to shrink back or even to want to disappear. Some people will even cover their faces, blush, and take a submissive stance in an attempt to withdraw.

The two most obvious directions that shame can take us is either to go outward with anger and blame or to go inward with depression and withdrawal. In the chapter on narcissism, we discussed the shame-prone person who gets angry and blames others, but shame can also drive us into isolation and the desire to avoid others. In this case the anger that is triggered by shame is directed inward, toward your own sense of self. This inwardly directed anger causes depression because anger is meant to be an energizing emotion that helps us solve problems. When it is directed toward your own sense of self, nothing is solved and you get a bottleneck of anger that is draining and eventually immobilizing. The result is depression that robs you of your motivation to do things, connect with others, or experience joy.

When people withdraw because of shame, they can become shy or afraid they are going to be exposed in front of a stranger. What they fear will be exposed is their feelings of self-doubt or worthlessness because of something negative they might do or say. This form of shyness is enhanced around strangers because we believe that since they don't know us, we are safe if we keep our vulnerable feelings hidden. This results in becoming easily embarrassed for fear of being seen as socially inadequate in some way.

When shame causes you to withdraw, you stagnate. Shame kills creativity and makes it difficult to learn new things, be innovative, or grow. Sadly, shame-prone withdrawal causes us to disconnect from the very source of our healing—relationships with God and others. Some people develop an attitude of scarcity, which makes it very difficult to be a productive member of any community. This can easily result in people becoming marginalized and lonely—or even worse.

Our psychological and spiritual lives are more important than our physical lives. That is, if we feel so withdrawn because of chronic shame that we doubt the value of our lives, we will do anything to make these feelings go away. Some people go so far as to hurt themselves in a desperate attempt to stop the painful feelings of shame. One example of this is when people cut or mutilate their bodies to try to change the way they feel. For them, this is an attempt to control the uncontrollable feelings of shame. If my arm hurts because I cut it with a razor, I am distracted from the pain in my heart of feeling that I don't belong. For other people, cutting or hurting their own bodies is an attempt to feel alive again, because the chronic shame they have been living with has caused them to become numb, or feel dead inside. Causing themselves pain is a way to feel alive again, even at the expense of threatening their own physical health.

What is even more extreme is when a person goes so far as to attempt suicide in an effort to stop the pain. The pain that a person must be in to drive them to this point is unimaginable if you have never felt it. But it is powerful nonetheless—so powerful that some people choose to stop their physical lives to escape the pain of their emotional lives. You may have thought that self-preservation is a powerful human motivation, but physical self-preservation is not the most powerful one. The gut-wrenching pain of shame-prone withdrawal can be so devastating that some people will do anything to make it go away. We were not made to be disconnected from God and others. Suicide is one of the most dramatic examples of what people are willing to do to escape the hell they experience because of it.

After having said all of this, I need to add a caveat about shyness. Not all shyness is caused by shame. Some shyness is a result of introversion, which is a personality style, not a psychological problem. Our society privileges extroversion over introversion, which I believe is a mistake. Other cultures consider extroversion arrogant and rude, and sometimes this can be true. But neither extroversion nor introversion is healthier than the other; they are simply different personality styles. Shyness is not necessarily a problem; withdrawing from others out of shame is. It's important to know the difference.

ADDICTIONS

Elsewhere I have described addictions as a modern-day form of idolatry.[2] Addictions result when we substitute a *thing* for a relationship with God and others. The thing can be anything, because we can be addicted to anything. But we can only find meaning and joy in relationships, and we can't have a joyful relationship with a thing. A thing may give us the illusion of satisfaction, especially if it is mood altering, but this is only an illusion that eventually fades with time. The longing for satisfaction forces us to go back to the altar of the thing we worship; only now we need more of it to keep the illusion alive.

Understanding the relationship between addictions and shame is vital. We haven't scientifically discovered the reason some people are more vulnerable to addictions than others, but we know they are. We know that abuse, trauma, and a lack of proper emotional care make people vulnerable to addictions. Nevertheless, some people still fall prey to addictions even when none of these things are present in their lives. A biological explanation for addiction may exist that will allow us to formally call it a disease, and scientists will probably keep working on it until they find it. Even if we haven't discovered the "addiction gene" yet, thinking of it as a disease is a useful way to try to help those who suffer from it.

No matter what the cause of addictions, I can tell you that after having worked with addicts of many kinds over the years, I have observed one thing in common with all of them—chronic shame.

True addicts are people who cannot stop their addictions on their own. They differ from people who have *a problem* with substance abuse or addictive behavior. People who are problem drinkers (or users, gamblers, sexual misbehavers, etc.) have more control over their behavior. Addicts are in a different category. They become so committed to their addictive behavior that they are willing to lie, cheat, and steal to keep it going. They act in utterly immoral ways and deny the damage they cause to others because of it. Few things can make normal persons act in completely depraved ways more than addiction. And for that, addicts have a deep feeling of shame.

If we act in ways that hurt and even destroy our relationships, we are violating our very purpose for being. When addicts do this, they are doing violence to their very sense of self. Addicts cannot truly love others, or themselves, if they violate their created purpose for being. If they persist in this behavior, they eventually have to grow numb inside. They feel numb to the pain they cause others, numb to the emptiness they feel as a result of substituting a thing for relationships, and numb to the worthlessness that results from rejecting the way they are created to be. Tragically, what addicts do to deal with this state of affairs is turn to the medication of their addictions to keep themselves numb. It doesn't really make them feel better, but it does temporarily keep them numb to their shame.

When anyone chooses to numb themselves, they are taking a step *away* from relationships. This isn't just true for addicts; it is true for all of us. Numbing keeps us from being vulnerable to others, which shields us from painful feelings. But numbing ourselves cannot change our behavior; it won't change our thinking, and it can't change how we feel about ourselves. That kind of transformation can happen only in relationships with God and others. Numbing ourselves doesn't do anything to help our loneliness or shame. For addicts, it just perpetuates those things.

If you can identify some addictive behavior in your life, you may be feeling a little nervous right now. But let me offer you some comfort by saying that the important thing to consider at this point is not so much *what* you are doing but *why* you are doing it. Two people can be doing the same thing, and for one it is addictive behavior that is intended to cover over shame while for the other it is not.

The apostle Paul alludes to this in passages like "It is better not to eat meat or drink wine or to do anything else that will cause your brother or sister to fall" (Romans 14:21). For some new believers in his day, eating meat used in pagan sacrifice or drinking wine was offensive, so rather than offend them because of what this behavior meant to these young Christians, it was better for the mature believers not to do it even if it didn't mean anything to them. His point was the same one I want you to consider now: It is not so much what you are doing at times but why you are doing it that matters. No substance is inherently addictive, but any substance can be used as an addiction. And when it is, you will be dealing with shame.

To determine whether you have addictive behavior, you need to ask yourself some hard questions. Are you substituting a thing for a relationship? Are you doing things to numb yourself to cover over painful feelings? Are you engaged in any behaviors that might be a way to hide feelings of shame? These are important things to consider, especially because we live in a culture that is widely committed to numbing itself. This is not very hard to see. Just look around.

PANIC ATTACKS

It goes without saying that shame-proneness causes anxiety. If negative events trigger the belief that you don't belong, you are going to feel anxious. If this happens often, you may even have anxiety attacks or bouts of anxiety that are disturbing to you. But an even deeper level of distress can result from chronic shame—panic attacks. These are not just bouts of anxiety; they are overwhelming physiological events that make you think you are going to die.

A panic attack is a sudden episode of intense fear that triggers physical reactions that can be very debilitating. It causes a person to feel as if they are losing control or having a heart attack. Most people don't have panic attacks, and most of those who do only have them once or twice in a lifetime. But some people suffer from multiple panic attacks on a regular basis, which can be a very difficult way to live.

Panic attacks come on suddenly without warning. They are physically very exhausting and frightening, even though they cannot actually harm you. If you have ever had a panic attack, it is unmistakable. You are filled with a sense of impending danger; your heart races, hands sweat, and body trembles; you can't catch your breath; your throat tightens; your chest hurts; you get hot flashes or chills; you become dizzy and feel a numb or tingling sensation; and you develop a headache. In short, a panic attack simulates a heart attack and you think you are going to die. That is why many people rush to the emergency room fearing for their lives. Panic attacks won't kill you, but you won't believe this when it's happening.

I could say quite a bit about panic attacks, what causes them and how to treat them, but the aspect I want to point out here has to do with their relationship to shame. As I said, most people who have panic attacks only have one or two in an entire lifetime. But the people who suffer from them regularly have an additional problem to face—chronic shame.

People who suffer from recurring panic attacks have developed an intense fear of them. They are horrible and terrifying, so

why someone would fear having another one is completely under-
standable. However, this then becomes its own problem. Once
you develop a fear of panic attacks, you then become afraid of anxiety. Unfortunately, anxiety is a part of life and cannot be elimi-
nated from normal daily activities. So when something happens
that makes you anxious, you instantly become afraid you are going
to have another panic attack, so you go on high alert trying to avoid
what you fear is about to become another debilitating and frightening experience. And what does all this effort do? It makes you
more anxious. This, then, makes you more afraid and intensifies
your battle to rid yourself of your anxiety. This battle within yourself (which can take place in a matter of seconds) plays an instrumental role in the very thing you are desperately trying to avoid—a
panic attack.

Most people who suffer from regular panic attacks are somewhat
aware of this self-defeating cycle of fear and anxiety, but they often
are not aware that this cycle is rooted in a chronic feeling of shame.
People with continual panic attacks have a deep feeling of failure
that they are not a strong enough person to control their feelings.
They feel they should be able to stop the panic attacks, but they are
just too weak to do it. This makes them feel defective, embarrassed,
and humiliated by the loss of control that panic attacks bring.

So the truth is that chronic panic attack sufferers are not only
afraid of anxiety but ashamed to be *the kind of person* that cannot
control it. This makes the treatment of panic attacks all the more
difficult, because once you add the element of shame-proneness to
the mix, you have made the vulnerable exploration of the feelings
involved with panic attacks much more challenging. Shame makes
us want to hide our feelings, not bring them out into the open for
healing. Shame makes us feel unworthy of love and connection, the
very things that can help us feel comforted and soothed. Chronic

shame is depressing, which is exactly what people who suffer from panic attacks don't need.

In working with people who suffer from panic attacks, I have learned that dealing with the shame-proneness that comes with them is crucial. Trying to control your anxiety typically just makes you feel bad about yourself when you find it impossible to do it. Becoming aware that your fear and shame are bigger problems than your anxiety is usually the way out of the panic attack cycle. Fearing your anxiety and feeling shame for having it only makes it worse. Developing the belief that anxiety is normal and nothing to be ashamed of plays a central role in healing this debilitating condition.

FUNDAMENTALISM

Religious fundamentalism has been the source of tremendous conflict throughout history, and this is no less true today than it has ever been. Some people are tempted to blame the problem on religion itself, but we can dig a little deeper into the subject and find some more helpful ways of understanding it.

Freud thought all religions were a defense against helplessness. He believed that religious people can't stand feeling powerless, so they make up the fantasy of an all-powerful God to save them from these intolerable feelings. The religious people he observed were defensive, rigid, and not self-reflective. I know some people like that, and I don't particularly like them either, but Freud's mistake was judging all religious people by the behavior of the ones who were acting badly. That wasn't very scientific of him.

Jesus didn't like defensive, rigid, and non-self-reflective religious people either. In fact, most of the harsh things he had to say were directed at religious types like that. He warned his followers to "be on guard" (Matthew 16:6) against the teaching of the Pharisees, and he called them "hypocrites" because "they do not do what they preach" (Matthew 23:3-13). You might say that Jesus was against all religion if you define his approach to God as based on a personal relationship rather than based on religious practices, but this isn't exactly fair to religion. James refers to a "pure and faultless" religion (James 1:26-27) in an honest attempt to make room for religion that is acceptable to God. I don't like to think of myself as religious because I prefer Jesus's emphasis on a personal relationship with God. But because I am a Christian, the fact remains that I practice the Christian religion. I am proud of the fact that Christianity as a religion has done more good for the planet than any other institution in history (and yes, I am aware of all the criticisms of it), so I don't want to throw the baby out with the holy water. Therefore, after years of study on this subject, I can tell you that from a psychological perspective, the problem is not with religion, it is with fundamentalism.

Fundamentalism is a mind-set.[3] You can be a fundamentalist about religion, politics, race, sex, values, or just about any set of beliefs. Psychologists have helped us understand this by separating dogma from dogmatism. You can be dogmatic about any dogma, because dogmatism is simply a rigid way of thinking. So what both Freud and Jesus were actually upset about in the religious people they encountered was not their religion per se but the dogmatic way they went about it. That's why Jesus said things like, "Do not think that I have come to abolish the Law or the Prophets; I have not come to abolish them but to fulfill them" (Matthew 5:17). Their dogma was not the problem; they just needed to not be so dogmatic that they couldn't see that he was the Messiah who had come to make their religion complete. Their religion wasn't their problem; their rigid thinking was.

And that brings me to my point. What makes someone a

fundamentalist? Why would anyone want to be rigid and defensive and refuse to be self-reflective? I doubt those are qualities to which anyone consciously aspires. You have probably guessed by now where I'm headed. That's right, once again the culprit is shame.

Brené Brown says, "Faith minus vulnerability equals politics, or worse, extremism. Spiritual connection and engagement is not built on compliance, it's the product of love, belonging, and vulnerability."[4] She sounds a lot like Jesus here when he said things like, "Woe to you, teachers of the law and Pharisees, you hypocrites! You travel over land and sea to win a single convert, and when you have succeeded, you make them twice as much a child of hell as you are" (Matthew 23:15). Ouch! Jesus understood that good religion is open, loving, and humble. Bad religion is closed, rigid, and absolutely certain of its own righteousness. And what makes a person want to hide, defend against imperfections, and refuse to be vulnerable? Shame.

Fundamentalism is actually a defense against shame. At their core, fundamentalists insist they are absolutely right as a defense against the fear that there is something very wrong with them. Fearing that they are not enough, they must insist they are more than adequate.

This is not a pretty picture. Religious fundamentalism is so uncomfortable for most of us that our first inclination is to turn our attention to the fundamentalists of other religions. They are easy to find because the news is full of them. But I think it is more useful for us to turn this scrutiny on ourselves here, in part because blaming others is actually a sign of shame hidden within ourselves. Despite the fact that fundamentalists in other religions are wreaking havoc in our world today, weeding out the rigidity and defensiveness that we have in our own Christian communities is still vital. The fundamentalism of other religions may be worse, but that doesn't make ours better.

Shame has many faces. I have listed a few of them in this chapter, but religious fundamentalism just might be the ugliest. Jesus spoke of love, service to others, and a joyful relationship with God. He was nonviolent and was willing to sacrifice his own life to show us that loving God and others is the better way to live. But sadly, over the two thousand years since he walked among us, a number of fundamentalists have done some awful things while claiming to be Christians. You see, one of the characteristics of the fundamentalist mind-set is that it is attracted to violence. The shame-prone core of fundamentalism results in a tendency to use anger destructively, and when you have the religious conviction that God is on your side, you can convince yourself that anything you do to combat the unfaithful is justified, even if that means hurting them.

While Christian fundamentalists have committed some acts of physical violence throughout history, those are not my focus here. The more pressing concern for you and me is not this form of extremism. The way the fundamentalist mind-set will show itself in your life or mine will be much subtler than that.

The most common danger you probably will have to face regarding fundamentalism is the temptation toward superspirituality. Despite the fact that you may have a very genuine relationship with God, when you suffer from shame-proneness you will find it very difficult to be simply spiritual; you will feel you must be superspiritual to cover over any doubts anyone might have about you. When this happens, the violence that you will be attracted to will most likely not be to physically hurt others but to damage them emotionally and spiritually instead. This form of superspirituality is the source of spiritual abuse that can be very hurtful, and it is not motivated by love of the truth but rather by fear of your own shame.

People who turn to superspirituality do so because they feel ashamed of their very sense of self. They live with the belief that they are flawed, spoiled, and defective; and so the only legitimate feeling to have about themselves is shame. To escape this state of being, they must believe that they are spiritually superior. This is a desperate attempt to numb themselves from the pain of having human needs and desires that are evidences of their defectiveness. Rather than vulnerably turn to God or the community of believers to find the love and belonging that could help them, they turn to superspirituality to reassure themselves that they will not be rejected for their flawed sense of self because they are more than acceptable as a result of their superspirituality.

God doesn't need you to be super anything. He just needs you to be you. He is the one who is more than adequate; you don't have to be. If you feel inadequate and are tempted to overcompensate spiritually, you may want to examine your heart for feelings of shame that may be motivating you. Because shame motivates us to hide, you will find it difficult to vulnerably acknowledge your fears that you are flawed, and because of this you don't belong. This is the opposite of what God wants for you. He wants you to honestly acknowledge that you are an imperfect person who will always fall short of the mark but are unconditionally loved by him anyway. Yes, because you are human you will always be a sinner, but God does not want you to live a shame-prone life because of this fact; he wants you to experience grace. Then you can honestly acknowledge that you are flawed and loved at the same time, not defective and destined to be rejected because of it.

As I mentioned earlier, being a member of the Christian church presents us with a kind of paradox. On the one hand, it is easy to misunderstand the apostle Paul as saying we should be sinless when he says things like we should be "children of God without fault in a warped and crooked generation" (Philippians 2:15). On the other hand, however, we are supposed to be so vulnerable that we can "confess [our] sins to each other" (James 5:16) without any embarrassment in doing so. Striving to be a good person while having the courage to admit that you are constantly falling short means you have experienced quite a bit of healing in the area of shame. While this may be difficult, it is not impossible. The good news is, God has given us the healing power of grace to deal with our shame. Sometimes we experience that grace coming directly from God, and sometimes we experience it in our relationships with one another. In the next two chapters, I'll explain the relationship between grace and shame to help you find the path to overcoming shame in your own life.

CHAPTER TEN

What's the Point of Therapy?

We have pretty well established that the major source of chronic shame is a lack of responsiveness from the important people in our lives. As infants, if we are looking up to see a smiling face beaming down on us and all we get is something like the *still face* in Dr. Tronick's experiments that I described earlier, we are well on the way to developing shame-proneness. And not only that, but we now know that children under age five will fail to thrive and even die if not physically held.[1] Our need for responsiveness is not just some warm and fuzzy psychological idea; our very lives depend on it. So in reality, the feeling of shame is the critically important emotional response to the breaking of the interpersonal bridge that our lives and well-being depend on. The reason shame hurts so much is because of the importance of our connections and our need to belong.

The natural temptation when considering the origins of shame, especially because it starts so early in life, is to blame our parents. After all, they were there when all of our problems got started. And that is exactly what many people do when they decide to come to therapy for help—blame their mothers.

Many people come to therapy with the belief that they are hiring me to relieve them of their guilt. Especially in America, we are supposed to be self-reliant, resilient, and certainly not needy. The hallmark of the life well lived is to be able to say, "I have no regrets," and therapy is the place we go to get over whatever bad feelings we may have about ourselves that don't belong in the life of a successful, well-adjusted person who has come of age. So people come to therapy with the attitude that I am supposed to help them identify their guilt, blame it on their mothers, and relieve them of any lingering regrets that might be getting in the way of their happiness. The problem with this is that the only people who truly have no regrets are psychopaths.

In America too many people believe vulnerability is the same thing as weakness, and that needing other people means you are needy. We are supposed to pull ourselves up by our bootstraps, shake off painful feelings, and never be dependent. Independence is an American value, and it permeates our collective psyche. Tragically, none of these things are consistent with the way we are made by God. Our purpose in life is to enjoy our relationships with God and others. This requires vulnerability, acknowledging our need for others, facing our suffering, and experiencing dependence as a strength, not a weakness. Guilt is the painful feeling we get when we have done something to hurt our relationships, and it alerts us to take action to mend whatever damage we may have done. Guilt is not your problem; shame is.

Therapy is not the place you go to be relieved of your guilt. It is where you go to be healed of your shame. Guilt is not associated with psychological problems. Even the most guilt-prone people among us are empathic and concerned about making repairs to broken relationships. They use their anger constructively, tend not to blame others, take responsibility for themselves, and avoid high-risk behaviors that can get them into trouble. You don't want to be relieved of your guilt, because guilt is not a problem.

WHAT'S THE REAL ISSUE NOW?

As I said earlier, the feeling of shame becomes a problem when that feeling unconsciously defines your sense of self. When the feeling of shame triggers the unconscious belief that you are unlovable, you develop a pattern of automatically responding with shame when negative events happen in your life. As I have pointed out several times, this is what Dr. Tangney call *shame-proneness*.[2] Now you not only *feel* worthless, but you believe you *are* worthless. Some psychologists have referred to this as the *internalization* of shame as opposed to the temporary feeling of shame. While this way of conceptualizing shame is handy, it commits the dualistic Cartesian error of splitting the human mind into a container that has an inside and the rest of the world that is outside of it.[3] This creates a picture that is easy to grasp, but it is not an accurate depiction of how human psychology actually works.

We don't internalize shame (as if it is something from the outside that we somehow swallow up inside of us); rather, we develop the belief that the feeling of shame is evidence that we are fundamentally flawed. The problem is that with enough disappointments in life, you will come to believe a lie about yourself. The lie is that every time you feel the feeling of shame, it reminds you that you are unlovable and less than others and that you don't deserve to belong. What's worse is that this belief is unconscious, which means you don't even know you are doing this. All you know is that when negative events happen, you feel bad about yourself. In many instances you don't even know the real reason why, but you feel bad anyway.

If you are in the grips of shame-proneness, you believe this unconscious lie about yourself. And because something in the unconscious is experienced as a fact, now you don't just *believe* you are worthless, you *know* you are. This is why many people come to therapy already discouraged. They know they can't change the past, and yet they know that somehow their struggles in the present began there. They often believe they can't get what they need now. The time for getting what they needed from their parents is past; it's too late now to do anything about that. So they come for help in the grips of the belief that help is not really possible.

While you cannot change the past, you can change how you feel about yourself in spite of it. And that is all that matters when it comes to shame. If you come to therapy with me, we will talk about your mother. However, we will talk about your childhood so we can understand what happened to you, not to blame it on your mother, but so *you* can take responsibility for it and make the changes you need to make now. When people say to me, "I don't want to waste a lot of time complaining about my childhood. I don't like to look back," I can only reply, "If you don't understand your history, you are doomed to repeat it."

The main reason people struggle emotionally is because of wounds from the past. Perhaps you didn't get the responsiveness you needed, or maybe you didn't get physically or emotionally held at the times that were most important, or maybe you were abused at the hands of bigger people who had no regard for the damage they were causing you. These violations of safety and connection with others are the sources of our shame. If we have not been treated as valuable by important people in our lives, we will find it difficult to escape the feeling that we are not valuable ourselves.

Because none of us had perfect lives, all of us have shame, just to varying degrees. No matter how great your parents were, you experienced disappointments. And even if you believe your parents were perfect (like Adam and Eve's), you still would have mismanaged your shame because you weren't perfect (just like Adam and Eve). So we all have doubts about our worth at times, we all fear we don't deserve to belong in certain situations, and we all feel we are not enough (or too much) for someone else. And because shame makes us want to hide, we often don't see how central it is to our problems. It compromises our ability to be empathic, causes us to blame others, inhibits vulnerability, and underlies many of the bad decisions we make. Shame is often the real issue for us; we just don't usually know that when it's happening.

WHY SOME PEOPLE MISUNDERSTAND THE POINT OF THERAPY

To be fair, people come to therapy for all kinds of reasons. Some have inherited a biological predisposition to psychological problems that destined them to struggle emotionally from the moment they were born. These people would be coming to therapy for help no matter what kind of childhood they had. But the people who come to therapy for the purpose of getting rid of their guilt may be missing the point. Even the people who come to therapy because of chronic guilt suffer from excessive guilt only because they don't see their problem with underlying shame. So what is it that therapy can do to help people with their shame? How do they find healing? Well, one way of explaining it is to put it in terms of self-punishment.

If your real issue is shame, you have judged yourself as someone who is disqualified from being loved. This results in a pattern of bad choices that can be understood as a form of self-punishment. People who unconsciously believe they are worthless cannot help but make choices that are consistent with that belief. They act badly because they believe they are bad, even if that belief is out of their conscious awareness. The only way out of this battle with themselves is to find freedom from the pattern of self-punishment. To put it simply, people who overcome their shame do so when they are able to have *mercy* for themselves.

MERCY FOR ONESELF

As I mentioned earlier, justice is the process of judging which punishment is appropriate for each crime. Lesser crimes get lesser punishment—that's how all civilized societies work. Mercy is releasing someone from punishment even though that person deserves it. When James says, "mercy triumphs over judgment" (James 2:13), he is telling us that the system of judgment that Jesus brought to us is the only one that can truly give us freedom, because his is based on grace.

Mercy applies to your relationship with others, but it can also apply to your relationship with yourself. You have done things that you are not proud of, and at times you have even been angry at yourself for having done those things. If you responded with guilt, you may have taken action to make amends for the things you did. But if your response was shame, you may be dragging a list of things around with you that have now turned into evidence that you use to convict yourself of past crimes. If you are holding yourself hostage for past bad behavior, then you are probably not just feeling guilty; you are struggling with shame. People who can't let go of the past are not upset because they did bad things; they are upset because they use those things as evidence to prove they are bad people. If you are one of those people, you are at war with yourself, and that is a battle you cannot win.

You can be your own worst enemy. If you are shame-prone, you live with the conviction that you are somehow defective, or a broken person. When bad things happen, you use those bad things as evidence that this previously held conviction is true. You are like a lawyer who is already convinced of the outcome of the trial before it happens, and as soon as you find evidence that supports your conclusion, you latch onto it with "Aha! See, I knew it was true!"

Shame-prone people punish themselves for failing to be the person they should be but aren't. You have a standard you are failing, and if you are shame-prone, you use that failure to support your shame. This leads to self-defeating behaviors, bad choices in relationships, and a long list of psychological problems. Because shame makes you want to hide, you don't learn anything new about yourself. You just keep coming to the same conclusion over and over again: You failed, so you are a failure.

This is where therapy comes in. The goal of good therapy is to uncover the truth about who you were created to be and how you came to be the person you are today. First we work on understanding what happened to you and what you believe about yourself because of it. If you are shame-prone, we will expose the lie that you are unlovable and inferior to others, and that you don't deserve to belong, which is the basis of your shame. Once this lie is brought into conscious awareness, you will have a new experience of it. Unconscious lies are experienced as facts that cannot change, but once they become conscious, they take on the quality of a subjective belief. Before when negative things happened, you *knew* you were not worthy of love; now you will be able to say that you have always *believed* this to be true, but fortunately, unlike facts, beliefs can change.

Once you are aware of the lie that you are not worthy of love, you will be able to piece together the things that happened in your life to help you understand how you came to believe in it so strongly. You developed strategies in childhood to survive the difficulties there, and now you will be able to judge for yourself whether you want to continue on with these same strategies in your adult life. Many of them were based on coping with shame's lie, and you can now ask yourself whether you want to keep fighting that fight over and over again.

It is at this point that you will have a powerful opportunity to release yourself from the pattern of self-punishment that has held you captive for years. When all the evidence is carefully weighed and you have come to see why you are the way you are, you will have the opportunity to judge for yourself the punishment you truly deserve. Should you continue on punishing yourself based on the lie that you are not worthy of love, or will you have mercy for yourself instead? The choice will be yours. True, you are guilty of past failings. But will you release yourself from the punishment you think you deserve, or will you have compassion on yourself with a new understanding you never had before?

Jesus said, "Go and learn what this means: 'I desire mercy, not sacrifice'. For I have not come to call the righteous, but sinners" (Matthew 9:13). He was not interested in piety or striving for ideal standards of living. People who are shame-prone condemn themselves for failing to be righteous. They mistake the point of life (and therapy) as a struggle against imperfections, so they try to numb themselves from the pain of their secret defectiveness with all sorts of addictions and enactments. And for some, sadly, coming to therapy is one of them. Yes, some people come to therapy to try to hide from their shame. They want me to explain to them how they can make the right "sacrifices" to achieve the psychological righteousness they know exists out there somewhere, which they believe will rid them of their shame. "Just tell me what to do, and I'll do it," they say to me, as I try to point them in the direction of mercy and grace.

It's not your fault you are the way you are; but it is your fault if you stay that way. Who you are today is a combination of your inherited physical makeup and all of your experiences in life up until now. You couldn't control most of what happened to you growing up, but you can work on understanding the impact it had on you and take responsibility for doing something about it now. That's why we talk about your mother in therapy. Not to blame her, but so that you can understand why you are the way you are and take responsibility for it. Will you keep on punishing yourself with your shame-proneness, or will you have mercy on yourself based on everything you now know? The goal of therapy is to help you choose mercy.

Kim Grew Up in an Unhappy Home

The term *unhappy home* should be an oxymoron, but sometimes it isn't. Sadly, Kim can tell you exactly what it means. She was an afterthought in her family, a surprise that came late in life for her parents, who already had three kids and could barely make ends meet. They hadn't planned to have another child, so she was what most people refer to as an "accident." And this is exactly what Kim felt about herself throughout her childhood.

Kim was pleasant enough, as children go who were not wanted, but she never had a solid sense of belonging. She wasn't extroverted, so she wasn't one of the popular kids. She wasn't athletic, so she didn't fit in with that crowd either. And while Kim was pretty intelligent, she didn't have the confidence or study skills to maximize her potential in school. Kim was one of those kids who hid in the background hoping not to be noticed. She didn't act up, so she didn't get in trouble with teachers, but she didn't stand out, so she didn't get their attention or praise either.

All of this would not have been so bad if things at home had gone well for Kim, but unfortunately that just wasn't the case. Kim's family considered themselves to be good Christian people. They went to church, didn't drink alcohol, rarely used bad language, and tried to live upstanding moral lives like the Bible said they should. Looking back on it, Kim believes her parents were Christians; they just weren't the joyful kind. Kim's mother was passive and distant, so Kim never felt very close to her. Kim believed her mother was not a bad person, but she was pretty sure that her mother wasn't very close to anyone, including her father.

Kim's father believed that respect was more important than happiness, and that obedience was more important than feelings (or love, for that matter). He was strict and critical, so she spent most of her time around him trying either to please him or avoid him. Anytime he did notice her, it was to point out something she could do better. On the surface it might have looked like he was trying to help Kim be a better person, but it didn't feel that way to her. To Kim her father's criticisms were not rooted in an attempt to help her do better but were more motivated by his need to look better himself. He appeared very concerned about what other people thought of him and his family, and her father-daughter conversations with him were never dialogues, but monologues directed at getting her to be more of the daughter he needed her to be.

Kim spent a lot of time in her room growing up. It seemed like the safest place to be. Sometimes she would crouch down next to the window and read a book. She could hide in the curtains there hoping no one would see her while she felt the warmth of the sun coming in the window. It was the only genuine source of warmth she could remember growing up. Her parents certainly weren't warm, so she never even tried going to them for comfort.

The first time Kim felt attracted to a boy she was about eleven. She remembers thinking about him quite a bit and developing elaborate fantasies about a growing closeness between them. She didn't know much about sex, so her fantasies were actually more romantic than anything else. Unfortunately, her older brother somehow figured out that she had a crush on the neighbor boy, and he did what almost all older brothers do in these situations: He teased her.

"Kim and Bobbie sitting in a tree K-I-S-S-I-N-G," he taunted.

Kim will never forget it. Not just because her brother teased her, but because her whole family joined in by mocking her in one way or another. Her father told her she was not allowed to date, so she was not to get any ideas like that in her head. Her other brothers gleefully ridiculed her for even thinking anyone would be interested in their younger sister, especially since they considered her such a social misfit. And her mother said nothing. As you know, sometimes that's the most damaging response of all.

The soul of shame is the belief that you are not worthy of love, something is defective about you, you are less than others, and you don't belong. That is exactly what Kim felt for years, and the incident with Bobbie confirmed it for her. Both consciously and unconsciously Kim organized her very sense of self around the belief that she was not worthy of love. The heartbreaking result was that she became shame-prone at a very early age.

By the time Kim got to high school, she was painfully convinced that the normal children would never accept her. She believed she was different, and not in a good way. Whenever she thought about boys, or the possibility of dating them, she would get this sick feeling in her stomach. She liked the idea of going out on a date, or maybe even going to the prom like "normal" kids do, but she had lost all her romantic feelings about the opposite sex. She wouldn't know what to do if a boy was interested in her, and she couldn't escape the feeling that *that just wasn't for her*. Maybe when she was younger, but not now. Eventually Kim began to wonder if she was even attracted to the opposite sex at all. I mean, if her father and brothers were any example of what men were like, she felt she could do just fine without them. To get to the point, Kim started to think that she was gay.

I know this is an extremely difficult subject to address, and I do not mean to imply that everyone has sexual feelings in the same way, especially in the overly sexualized world in which we live these days. I am talking specifically about Kim and the way her sexual feelings came about in her life. Other people will have a different story to tell, and I do not mean to suggest that their story is invalid just because it is different from Kim's. But the story I am relating to you about Kim is a true one, so I hope others will accept hers as valid even if it is different from theirs.

When Kim eventually made her way to therapy as an adult, she was a tortured woman. I have to say it was pretty impressive that she wanted to work with me, because I'm a man. She had been in therapy before with women, and now she wanted to try something different. She talked often of her guilt for having feelings of attraction toward the opposite sex, but I could see easily that her real problem was with shame. In Kim's case she wasn't attracted to homosexual women, but she was extremely attracted to women who weren't. She had a long history of developing intense romantic feelings for women she knew were not gay, and on a few occasions these feelings even became known to the women themselves. Sometimes the women would reject her harshly for being "weird," but many times they seemed quite tolerant of her affection toward them. Kim never really wanted to be in an ongoing sexual relationship with another woman; she just wanted to know that women she admired would find her attractive. If the cool normal girls were attracted to her, maybe she could be cool and normal too. It's just that having feelings of attraction for someone who doesn't have those feelings for you doesn't work very well. Tragically, Kim's romantic solution to her belief that she was unworthy of love just kept reinforcing her belief that she was unworthy of love.

"So do you have any feelings of attraction toward men?" I asked after we had been meeting for quite some time.

"No, I basically feel nothing," Kim replied. "I mean, I think I did once, you know, with Bobbie, and maybe before that. But not now."

"So then what is the feeling you get about women—the straight ones you have been telling me about?" I asked.

"A rush," she replied quickly. "I don't have that feeling for any man; in fact, I don't have that feeling anywhere else in my life. I can't help myself. It's like I have to have it, and I will scheme and manipulate other women until I get what I need."

There are two kinds of sexual feelings. The first is erotic love, which is the sexual feeling that God created to cement a marriage together (taken from the Greek word *eros*). God designed it to be the special feeling we get when we have a good relationship with a spouse we love. You can find out more about it by reading Solomon's Song of Songs if you like. But the other sexual feeling is eroticized love. This is the sexual feeling we get for someone with whom we don't have a good relationship and we are trying to substitute feelings of attraction for genuine love. Much of the entertainment industry as well as the multibillion-dollar pornography industry are based on this feeling. This is the sexual feeling we use to cover over our shame. You can read more about this in 2 Samuel 13 if you like.

Over time it became clear to Kim and me that the feelings of attraction she was having toward women were the eroticized kind. She had been so shamed as a young adolescent girl that she couldn't help believing the lie that she was defective—as a female. I'm sure her family didn't mean to do it, but she developed an unconscious belief about her sense of self that she was too defective to be the object of any man's attraction, and that she didn't belong among the *normal* group of girls. The rush she felt around them was like a drug that medicated her against the pain of her lifelong shame. She became so addicted to that rush that she grew numb to any feelings of attraction toward men. That was just too risky. Instead, she grew to define herself as a woman who was only attracted to other women; it's just that her preference was to be attracted to women who were attracted to men.

I don't think I know of anyone more courageous than Kim. She has been willing to show up each week to our therapy sessions and honestly confess her deepest and most shameful secrets over and over again. Many times I have been in awe of her courage and steadfast commitment to understanding herself. We have painstakingly gone over the events of her childhood many, many times. Each time we seek to understand what happened, how she felt about it, and the impact it has had on her today. You would think she would be angry at her parents for the damage they caused her, but surprisingly, she isn't. She believes what happened to her was wrong, but she has never been interested in blaming anyone for it. What she has been interested in is understanding what happened to her so she could eventually gain a new perspective on herself.

Kim used to believe she was disgusting. She doesn't feel that way anymore. Kim used to spend hours thinking of ways to get close to a woman who would give her a "rush." She hasn't had any interest in that for months now. Kim has avoided dating eligible men since age eleven. She is very cautiously developing a relationship with a Christian man who understands her and has no interest in "rushing" things. I don't mean to make this sound simple; it has taken us years to get to this place. But I believe the place we are in now is quite real, which is very different than living out of the lie that Kim has been in the grips of most of her life, the lie that she is not worthy of a man's love and that she doesn't belong among normal women.

I like to say that Kim has finally been able to have mercy for herself. She knows the things she has done, and she has lived for years with the notion that she deserves to be punished for the things in her heart. But now that all the evidence is in, and the jury of the two of us has deliberated on it for many years, she has come to a verdict. Her judgment is that she should release herself from the punishment she has unconsciously believed she deserved her entire life. Kim has been punishing herself with self-loathing and has mistakenly thought her central issue was guilt over sexual sin. Now she can see that her real issue has been with shame, and she is learning to have compassion on herself for believing a lie.

Kim's therapy with me is too complicated to explain fully, but what I can tell you is this: "Mercy triumphs over judgment" (James 2:13). Kim judged herself to be sick when in reality she was stuck. Kim judged herself to be guilty when her deeper issue was shame. Kim judged herself to be unworthy of love when nothing could be further from the truth. None of us deserves love, because all of us have failed in one way or another. But that does not mean we are not *worthy* of it. Kim's mercy for herself came in the form of compassion for a little girl who developed strategies for survival in a critical and shaming world. While those strategies may have hurt herself and others, she can release herself from the punishment she thought she deserved. I believe that Kim is a pretty powerful example of what it means to be merciful toward oneself, and someone who was able to come to understand the point of therapy.

THERAPY ITSELF CAN BE SHAMING

I need to add a couple of caveats here. First, choose your confidants wisely. To overcome your shame, you need to be vulnerable, but this requires wisdom. You may even need to go to therapy and open up your deepest, darkest secrets so that you can be understood and can pursue the path of mercy and grace. But just because you need to be vulnerable to someone doesn't mean you should be vulnerable to everyone. Therapy is designed to be a safe place to be vulnerable, but most other relationships are not designed that way.

Some people will be threatened by your vulnerability, and they may even attack you for it. Fortunately, most people will admire you for being vulnerable, even though few will join you there. Jesus is our model for everything, and he was willing to give his life as an example of how to love. He is an extraordinary model of vulnerability and strength. Remember, however, that such vulnerability comes with a price. You will need to weigh its cost and choose who will be able to respond to it and who won't.

That means you will need to choose your therapist wisely. Therapy is a very uneven or asymmetrical relationship. For it to work, you will have to be extremely vulnerable. Your therapist—not so much. Yes, your therapist should be trustworthy and genuine, but your therapist is not going to go into great detail about his or her mother and all the elements of shame that probably caused him or her to go into the profession of psychology in the first place. That wouldn't be appropriate, and I would politely refuse to go back to see any psychotherapist who did overdisclose about all those things. It's *your* therapy, so you are the one who is going to be most vulnerable, and feelings of shame may trigger when your therapist does not respond with the same level of vulnerability that you are courageously willing to share.

So you need to be able to talk with your therapist about your discomfort with the therapy process. If your therapist is blaming you or is judgmental, then you are going to need to talk about that and possibly choose another therapist if you can't resolve it. Some therapists will not be a good fit for you. Therapy is a mutual relationship, but it is not equal. This means you will mutually affect each other, but the power differential is always in the therapist's favor. Therapists choose what to disclose and when because it works best when they don't talk about themselves very much. This lack of equality is necessary for the process to work, but it is understandably shaming at times. You may feel shut out by your therapist's silence about his or her personal life, and that can feel as rejecting as Tronick's Still Face Experiment. That is a part of the process, and you must be prepared to talk about it. That part your therapist should be willing to do.

CHAPTER ELEVEN

Overcoming Shame

Shame is a moral emotion. It reminds us that we are not God. That's a good thing. However, shame-proneness does not help people act morally. That's a bad thing. In fact, people who are shame-prone are more aggressive, less empathic, blame others more frequently, and are less likely to make repairs in their relationships when there are problems.

Guilt is also a moral emotion. It reminds us when we have done something hurtful. But unlike shame-prone people, even those among us who are the most guilt-prone are more likely to be concerned about the harm they cause others, be more empathic, and look to repair whatever damage they may have caused others whenever possible. The feeling of guilt and the chronic condition of guilt-proneness are just not that bad. The only real problem we have with the moral emotions of guilt and shame seems to be restricted to the long-term effects of shame. That is where we need healing.

Professor Louis Smedes told us that feeling joy is the alternative to feeling shame.[1] We were created for joyful relationships with God and one another in the Garden of Eden, and that is where we have been trying to get back to since the moment we got kicked out. You cannot earn joy, and you cannot create it. It rarely comes through grand gestures or heroic efforts, and it usually comes in the simplest and most normal of circumstances. Joy is its own reward, and Professor Smedes reminded us that it is not something you feel when the world is working right, because the world never works right. To feel joy you must be primed to let it in, and to do that you must overcome your shame.

HEALING SHAME

I don't like the word *cure*. It implies being free of symptoms through the complete removal of disease. When you are cured, you are done. You don't have to worry about whatever ailed you ever again. I prefer the word *heal*, which implies the restoration of sound functioning with the goal of wholeness. Spiritually speaking, our goal is maturity—not a static state of perfection. We don't get cured in this life because we don't get done growing, but we can make mature growth our goal. You will never be completely cured of your shame, but you can pursue wholeness in your relationships with God and others. That is what I mean when I talk about healing your shame.

Brené Brown has studied this healing extensively.[2] Her research is so compelling that it has resonated with millions of readers around the world. We all are struggling with shame and desperately trying to figure out what to do about it. After years of study, she has concluded that empathy is the antidote to shame. Not just *understanding* someone, but connecting to the *emotions* of the other that sends the message "You are not alone."[3]

And to do this, Brown is convinced that we must be vulnerable. Vulnerability produces self-worth, and self-worth inspires vulnerability. Put simply, shame makes us want to hide and vulnerability is the opposite of that. Of course, few people truly want to be vulnerable.

That is where we get hurt, rejected, and most easily shamed. It's kind of a contradiction. We have to do the very thing that our shame makes us not want to do to heal our shame. So what does it take to do that? Courage. Brown says that to be empathic we must have the courage to be vulnerable. There is no other way to overcome our shame.

For some time now, I have been employing the research of people like Brené Brown and June Tangney in my clinical work. Recognizing shame-proneness and its toxic effect on the people who come to me for help has been extremely beneficial. Creating a safe space for people to be courageously vulnerable has been one of my main goals, and I have witnessed many people become more empathic and find healing because of it. However, as I paid extremely close attention to the stories I heard over the years, I noticed something else, something that I believe other clinicians—who are not researching shame but are trying to heal it in their consultation rooms—have observed. Courage and vulnerability are not enough. You might say they are necessary but not sufficient to overcoming shame. One of my most articulate patients put it as clearly as anyone could when she said to me, "I am one of the most vulnerable people I know, and I still struggle with shame." So what is the missing piece? Grace.

Professor Smedes, a theologian, said it best when he wrote, "The healing of our feelings of shame gets its best start with a spiritual experience—specifically, an experience of amazing grace."[4] *Grace* is the theological word for acceptance. In the deepest form, it means acceptance from God, and that is the most profound experience of healing anyone could ever have for shame. But grace applies to the acceptance we extend toward one another and to ourselves as well. To experience acceptance, courage and vulnerability are necessary, but without acceptance, you are only going to be courageously vulnerable all by yourself. Vulnerability in a vacuum doesn't heal your shame; vulnerability that is responded to with grace does.

Even though I am a clinical psychologist, I like to think of myself as a practical theologian.[5] I am helping the people who come to me apply the spiritual truths of Scripture (and the psychological wisdom found there) to their everyday lives, and in doing so they find the joy and meaning that they were created to experience more fully. And the single greatest need of anyone is the experience of grace. Grace is the acceptance God offers us, not because we deserve it, but because we are worthy of it. By virtue of being created in God's image, we are worthy of a relationship with him—a relationship that he is ready to extend to us if we are vulnerable enough to accept it. And once we experience grace, it changes us. It heals us of our loneliness, gives meaning to our otherwise directionless lives, grounds us in the joyful relationship we have always longed for, and finally, heals us of our shame.

Believing in acceptance requires faith. To experience acceptance, you must believe you are worthy of it. But as you know, shame-proneness is rooted in the unconscious belief that you are not worthy. Brené Brown says the people who live with a sense of worthiness are quite simply the people who *believe* they are worthy of it. So the real problem with shame is a spiritual problem. You believe the lie that you are not worthy, and the only way that lie can change is through an experience of grace that contradicts it. I can't just tell you that you believe a lie about yourself that is out of your conscious awareness; you must experience something new about yourself that is more powerful than the lie.

THE RENEWAL OF YOUR MIND

The apostle Paul instructed us, "Do not be conformed to the pattern of this world, but be transformed by the renewing of your mind" (Romans 12:2). He was talking about the ongoing power of the grace of God to transform us spiritually, but he was also making a brilliant statement about what happens to us psychologically when we experience grace. Shame is the feeling that there is something wrong with us that makes us unworthy of love—it makes us feel that we don't belong. An encounter with grace gives us the experience that we do.

As you now know, shame-proneness results from the unconscious belief that our very sense of self is worthless. This unconscious belief then gets triggered repeatedly when negative events happen, stimulating the repetitive feeling of shame and the inner conviction that we are bad and to blame. Because this is out of conscious awareness, it happens automatically, and it is very hard to change—but not impossible.

The bad news is that you cannot remove unconscious beliefs. They are neural pathways that get laid down in your brain and are there permanently. They can't be erased, and you can't be cured of them. The good news is that you can lay down new neural pathways that contradict the old ones, and if you use these new neural pathways often enough, they can become the more dominant and preferred ones. Over time the old pathways fade and get stimulated less often, and the new ones take on a life of their own. My point is, you cannot remove old unconscious beliefs, but you can create new ones. Psychologically, this is what happens when the experience of grace is renewing your mind.

In other words, if you are shame-prone you learned to believe the lie that you are not worthy and that you don't belong every time you feel the feeling of shame; but you can learn to believe something new. As you become consciously aware of your old unconscious lie, it changes. Now you are able to say, "I was convinced for most of my life that I was worthless when bad things happened, but now I can say that I'm not so certain that this is really true." Facts can't change, but beliefs do.

This is where grace comes in. The feeling of acceptance is not an intellectual idea; it is a personal experience. Shame-proneness results from damaging experiences that cause us to believe we are worthless; grace is a powerful experience of acceptance that heals this damage. The rational brain cannot heal shame because shame is not a cognitive distortion; it is an emotion that can get organized by unconscious beliefs that are outside of our rational control. To overcome shame you cannot just *do* something different; you must *be* something different. You must experience the renewing of your mind.

COURAGE, VULNERABILITY, AND ACCEPTANCE

So here is the formula for overcoming shame: *courage, vulnerability, and acceptance.* Coming out from behind your defensive strategies that protect you from the humiliating effects of shame takes courage. But if you are vulnerable in just the right circumstance with just the right people, you have the opportunity to experience the life-changing power of acceptance that can heal your shame. Courage and vulnerability are not enough. Because if you are vulnerable with the wrong people at the wrong time, you can be devastatingly humiliated and have your shame deepened, making you regret that you were ever that vulnerable in the first place. Choose your confidants wisely. Grace offered graciously heals, but grace offered ungraciously shames.[6]

To overcome shame you must be a gracious person toward others as well as toward yourself, and you must have gracious people around you to support living this type of courageous life. For some people this starts in psychotherapy where they learn to have mercy for themselves. In understanding how they came to be the way they are, they are able to bring their unconscious beliefs out into the light of day where lies can be exposed and new beliefs can be established.

But even this can happen only within the context of an accepting relationship where they can learn to accept themselves. For others this courageous life of grace will come in different forms. Perhaps they will find a mentor who offers them grace when they need it most, a teacher who understands them best, or a pastor who cares for them unlike anyone ever has before. Or maybe they will experience acceptance in a small group that allows for a deep level of vulnerability, or grow up with a best friend who is their lifelong confidant. One thing is certain: To overcome shame a person must experience acceptance at a time when they don't deserve it but need it more than anything else.

Shame-proneness can be healed only by the renewing of your mind, and that can happen only by experiencing acceptance of the unacceptable. By acknowledging your feelings of shame, you can open the door to healing them. If you can feel shame but experience acceptance precisely when you believe you don't deserve it, a new belief about your worthiness gets established. If you can feel grace when you believe you are unworthy, the meaning of the feeling of shame can change. The next time you feel shame, you might be able to acknowledge it for what it is, a feeling of being less, not proof of your unworthiness as a person. Perhaps then you can name the feeling of shame but organize it as meaning that you are a vulnerable person who makes mistakes but who is still worthy of acceptance. The grace we extend toward one another has the power to heal shame. Feeling that you don't belong is not the same thing as actually not belonging. Grace teaches us the difference.

THE HEALING EFFECT OF SALVATION

For Christians the first experience of the grace of God marks a turning point in our lives. When Jesus said to Zacchaeus, "Today salvation has come to this house" (Luke 19:9), he was marking that moment in time as the beginning of a new life for him. For some of us it happened when we were quite young, so it is difficult to say what we experienced. But for those of us who first entered into a relationship with God as adults, the experience of conversion may have been quite dramatic. Some people feel radically changed by the initial experience of salvation, and this experience can be hard to explain to those who have no idea what you are talking about.

The Bible tells us that from the very moment we become Christians we are new creatures in a new creation (2 Corinthians 5:17). To be fair, the Bible also talks about salvation as something that happens at one point in time, is ongoing, and will happen at some point in the future.[7] So to say that you "got saved" is simplistic if you only mean it is something that happened at one point in your past, because you are also "being saved" and "will be saved" when Jesus comes again. I think you know what I mean. Some people become Christians, and they are gradually transformed throughout their entire lives into maturer and more loving individuals. Others have gone to a Billy Graham crusade, accepted Christ, and been dramatically changed almost instantly. What happened?

Well, the obvious answer is that God changed them. By the power of the Holy Spirit, God reached down and touched their hearts and made something new happen within them. When Jesus was trying to explain to Nicodemus the meaning of being *born again*, he said, "The wind blows wherever it pleases. You hear its sound, but you cannot tell where it comes from or where it is going. So it is with everyone born of the Spirit" (John 3:8). The spiritual experience of transformation is not something we can *define* with human terms; we can only *describe* it the best we can. It defies explanation. It is real, but it is beyond us to scientifically explain it. Just like the wind whistling through the trees, however, we can observe its effects and try to understand them.

I cannot tell you how God changes us, but I can tell you some of the effects of that change. And one of the most powerful results of experiencing God's grace is the healing of shame. All of us walk around with some degree of shame. We can't talk ourselves out of it or even have someone else explain to us why we shouldn't feel it. But what we can do is to be courageously vulnerable enough to open ourselves up to a God we don't understand and experience what it is like to feel complete acceptance down to our very core. Courage, vulnerability, and acceptance heal shame. And experiencing that with God heals it in the most powerful way.

The Rest of Donnie's Story

Most of the time we never hear the rest of the story about the lives of people we know. Childhood friends grow up and move away, colleagues change jobs, and mostly we just lose touch with people and they drift out of our lives. Decades later we often wonder, *What ever happened to Joe?* or *Where is Karen living now?* Thanks to the marvels of the Internet, I had the opportunity to find out the rest of the story for someone I knew as a child. I am grateful to God that Donnie reached out to me after forty years, because I couldn't be happier to find out how he is doing today. After finding me on Facebook, Donnie and I met in a restaurant to catch up on the past four decades of our lives. Most of us have a special connection with certain people in life, and Donnie was one of those people for me.

Donnie and I played football together in high school. We grew up in a small town where Friday night football games were the talk of the community. One of the things that stood out about Donnie was that even though he wasn't a particularly large kid, he was one of the coolest guys you would ever want to meet off the field but one of the hardest-hitting guys you would never want to meet on it. He would literally use his body like a spear to take down players twice his size. He was an award-winning athlete because of the fire in his belly, which sometimes made me wonder where that heat was coming from.

After high school I moved away and Donnie and I lost contact with each other. I saw him once after graduation, and I was concerned about the direction his life seemed to be taking. He grew his hair out, bought a Harley, and started running with a bunch of guys that drank alcohol and used drugs regularly. He would even go on runs with a local biker gang that was notorious for getting into trouble with the law, because that's where he could get the good stuff when he wanted to get high.

Donnie had his eye on an attractive girl a few years younger than him who he thought was pretty special. He asked her out on a date and showed up on his Harley wearing a biker jacket and thinking he was looking pretty cool. Before she could go out with him, she told Donnie that her father wanted to speak with him in the kitchen in private. Not knowing what to expect, Donnie strolled into the kitchen to find her dad cleaning his gun at the kitchen table.

"Where you going with my daughter?" her dad asked as he wiped down the barrel of his revolver.

"Just on a date," Donnie replied as respectfully as he could.

"What time you bringing her back?" her dad asked without looking up.

"Whatever time you like, sir," Donnie said with a gulp.

"Everything better be okay," her dad said looking up into Donnie's eyes.

"Yes, sir. It will," Donnie said as he backed out of the kitchen.

Donnie didn't date the girl again for three years. He wanted to, but he just wasn't sure he could get over the bar of her father's expectations. So Donnie focused on his job and tried to stay out of trouble the best he could when he partied with his drinking buddies. He was smoking dope regularly now and drinking daily. Working on his Harley was his favorite pastime. Even though he dated several other girls, he couldn't stop thinking about the one who had captured his attention, so three years later he eventually asked her out again and they started dating regularly. One thing led to another, and without meaning to do it, Donnie and his girlfriend got pregnant. It shook him up quite a bit, not just because he was afraid of her father but because he wasn't sure what he was supposed to do now. Donnie grew up Catholic, so even though he had not been to church in years, he was pretty sure that abortion was a sin. He was never a bad person; he had just gotten lost when it came to spiritual and moral direction.

Feeling confused, Donnie went to one of his friends whom he knew had a Bible. Maybe he could offer some insight into what he was supposed to do. They started getting together to see if they could find anything in the Bible about abortion, and as was their custom, they spent the evening smoking pot to ease Donnie's anxiety at the same time. As Donnie tells the story now, it was quite a sight. They would take hits off their joint as they were flipping through the pages of the Bible, honestly seeking wisdom for the greatest moral struggle Donnie had ever faced. Donnie found both what he was looking for and also wasn't looking for—all at the same time. Reading the Bible was helping him with his moral dilemma, but he now had this nagging feeling that something was missing in his life, but he didn't know what it was.

Then it happened. His friend learned that Billy Graham was coming to the Hollywood Bowl for a major celebration, and he thought that he and Donnie should go. What did he have to lose? There was something about reading the Bible that seemed so helpful to Donnie, so why not go and hear from an expert what the Bible was all about? Well, they did. And the rest is history. Donnie found out what the story of the Bible was that day, and he gave his life to Christ and found the missing piece that he didn't even know he was looking for. And from that moment on, Donnie was a changed man. He stopped abusing drugs and alcohol, dropped out of the biker gang, sold his Harley, married his girlfriend, kept the baby, and joined a church where he could find out more about this life-changing thing that had happened to him.

Doors started to open for Donnie in every area of his life. He joined a large union and worked his way up to its highest level. Each time he was given an opportunity for advancement, he felt like it was a gift from God. Over the next few years, he became one of the most respected leaders in his profession, and he was elected the head of his union for twenty years in a row. Everyone looked to him for wisdom and guidance. If there was a problem, Donnie was the guy to solve it. If there was a disagreement, all eyes were on him to bring the parties together. Donnie drove down to the Hollywood Bowl that day as a man who was lost and in search of something missing in his life; he drove home that same day as a changed man because he found it.

As I sat in the restaurant listening to Donnie's story that morning, I found myself wondering why I was so comfortable with him. It wasn't because we had a few beers to loosen up and cover over any anxiety we might feel for meeting up with someone we hadn't seen for forty years. We were drinking water. It wasn't because we had a long list of things in common so we could lose ourselves in all the memories we had shared over the years. We hadn't seen each other for decades. It wasn't because we were having so much fun or being crazy. We were having a mostly serious conversation about the meaning in our lives and how God had kept us alive for some purpose (each of us shared a few near-death stories). In fact, our conversation was so vulnerable for me that I teared up a few times during that lunch with Donnie (and remember, I listen to emotionally moving stories every single day). I was moved by his sincerity and how welcomed I felt in his presence. He had a strong sense of love and belonging. He didn't believe he deserved it, but he did believe that he was worthy of it. You can't earn this type of self-worth; either you have it or you don't. You *deserve* recognition for accomplishments, you *believe* you are worthy of love. I was in the presence of a man whose shame had been healed by the grace of God. He knew it, and I knew it too. Whatever the causes of the shame that drove him to numb himself with drugs, alcohol, and biker gangs in his earlier years had been, they were now gone. This was a man who no longer needed those escapes. He was grateful for the life he had and content in whatever circumstances he found himself. Here was a man living in joyful relationship with God and others, and I could not have felt more comfortable being right there with him.

Spiritually, God reached down and saved Donnie that day at the Hollywood Bowl. There is no other way to understand what happened to him. It took courage for him to go to the Bowl and vulnerability for him to ask God to take control of his life that day, and the experience of the grace of God for an undeserving but worthy man did all the rest. When Billy Graham asked Donnie if he wanted to accept Christ as his Lord and Savior that day, he was offering Donnie a chance for conversion. Donnie was presented with a chance to convert his life as a lost man, disconnected from God, to a man who now knew what he was looking for—a loving relationship with the creator of the universe for all eternity. But that is not the only thing that was converted that day. Donnie's shame, which he had been unsuccessfully trying to cover over with drugs, alcohol, and wild living and which he felt powerless to change, was converted into a feeling of guilt that he could do something about. When Donnie realized that he didn't have a relationship with God, he felt guilt. He had been living in a way that was hurting God, hurting others, and hurting himself. And for that he felt guilty. But as you know by now, guilt makes us want to do something to make things right. Guilt motivated Donnie to ask God for forgiveness for living the life he had been living, and opened him up to let God in to the deepest places of his heart that no one had ever visited before. Donnie realized that day the deepest reason why God created the feeling of guilt. It prompts us to make things right, not just with other people, but with God.

Psychologically, the grace of God healed Donnie of his shame that day at the Hollywood Bowl. His old unconscious beliefs surrounding his unworthiness were challenged by the life-changing experience of acceptance by a loving God. His salvation started that day. Now let me be clear, I believe Donnie had to stay on the right path for the healing of his shame to continue. If he had accepted Christ and then gone home to return to his former life, I believe Donnie's life would have turned out much different than it is today. I am not questioning the validity of his spiritual conversion that day, but I am certain that if he had not continued to surround himself with gracious people and continued to learn what it meant to be a gracious person himself, his shame-proneness would have returned. If you think about it, you probably know people yourself that turned out this way.

For years after that day at the Hollywood Bowl, Donnie would run into his old drinking buddies, and they would ask, "Hey, Donnie. Where have you been?" With a knowing smile, he would simply reply, "Oh, I've been right here all along. I just don't do that stuff anymore." Removing himself from environments where his old unconscious beliefs could be reinforced and seeking out new places where he could continue to experience grace solidified a new belief of worthiness that eclipsed the old unconscious lie he had been trying to escape before. Donnie's shame-proneness was healed by the grace of God, and it continues to be healed to this day because he is living a courageously vulnerable life surrounded by grace. No one gets cured of shame, but it can be healed. That means you, too, have to surround yourself with grace if you want new unconscious beliefs of worthiness to become more dominant than the old ones of unworthiness in your life. This is what it means to overcome your shame.

OVERCOMING SHAME

> Let us run with perseverance the race marked out for
> us, fixing our eyes on Jesus, the pioneer and perfecter
> of faith. For the joy set before him he endured the
> cross, scorning its shame, and sat down at the right
> hand of the throne of God.

HEBREWS 12:1-2

No person in all of history has made a greater impact on the world than Jesus Christ. Even those who would never refer to themselves as Christians point to his life as an example that anyone would do well to follow. His earthly life was the epitome of courage, vulnerability, and grace. He is the pioneer that goes before us, the one who has given us the perfect example to follow.

As you know, Jesus was crucified, which was such a humiliating form of punishment that all Roman citizens were exempt from this method of execution, as the state had determined it was reserved for only the subhuman races that were beneath them. But Jesus knew of a joyful existence that transcends all forms of shame. Nothing anyone could do to him could take this from him. Hanging there naked, abused, and suffering from society's most extreme attempt to shame him, he felt no resentment, no blame, and not even the slightest doubt about his self-worth. He was completely shame-free and convinced with every neuron in his brain that he was worthy of love and belonging. As he often did, he turned the situation on its head. He scorned shame. He made worthlessness worthless.

If you are like me, you did not have a conversion experience like Donnie's. Mine is pretty boring, and it took several years to take hold. But it doesn't matter. The point is, grace heals shame. Whether grace knocked you down and blinded you with its impact or snuck up on you over time, the experience of acceptance changes you. If you are willing to live a life of courage, vulnerability, and grace, you will be healing shame in your life and the lives of those around you. Jesus has paved the way before us. You will never live a shame-free life as he did, but you can set your sights on him as the pioneer who went before you to show you the way.

AFTERWORD:

The Differences Between Men and Women

We live in a very confusing time when it comes to sexuality. Psychiatrists once diagnosed homosexuality as a psychological disorder; now same-sex marriages are legal in all 50 states. For all of history, everyone assumed that you were either male or female, but today gender is not only considered a choice on most college campuses, but some people insist they can choose to be gender neutral if they want. The subject of the differences between men and women has become a political lightning rod, and an increasing number of people assert that it is simply politically incorrect to suggest that they exist. The problem with this is that we have plenty of sound scientific research that shows they do. I don't mean to be insensitive to those struggling with sexual identity issues, but I do believe that it is important to tell the truth about the differences between men and women when we have plenty of evidence that there are some. The differences noted here might not apply to some individuals, but with regard to men and women, they do pertain to the vast majority of us when it comes to shame.

Women consistently report more shame than men.[1] There are

several reasons for this. One might be that while women want to hear about other women's pain, they don't really want to listen to men when they talk about theirs.[2] Apparently when men speak of their pain, it seems like they are complaining, and women don't like that. Most women say they want men to be vulnerable, but the truth is they don't like it when men appear weak. And sadly, both men and women confuse vulnerability with weakness. Men are receiving a strange double message from women when it comes to shame and vulnerability. As it turns out, women *need* men to be vulnerable, but they also *want* them to be strong at the same time—which ends up meaning that neither women nor men want to listen to men talk about their shame. And what do men feel in response to this confusing message? Shame.

Women readily express sympathy, and men instinctively want to solve problems. Men are autonomous, and women nurture relationships. Women are shamed by attacks on their ability to relate to others, and men are shamed by put-downs and threats to their rank in social status. Women care about who is connected to whom, and men care about who is in charge.

When it comes to having sex, a man's self-worth is on the line. Sexual rejection is a major source of shame for men, which is a primary reason that men turn to pornography much more than women do. They don't have to risk sexual rejection there. Women mistakenly perceive the use of pornography by men as having something to do with a man's perception of the woman in his life as being somehow inadequate. This is rarely true. It has much more to do with a man's fear of being shamed by her sexual rejection of him. I think this same dynamic has a lot to do with the prevalence of violence and rape coming from men toward women, and the popularity of homophobia among men. A man with no sexual shame could believe homosexuality is wrong and have nothing to fear about taking this position. However, a man who has been sexually rejected to the point of shame-proneness might be forced to have a phobic response to men who are gay. Why else would they be so angry at homosexuals and afraid of appearing even the slightest bit homosexual themselves? As you know, shame-proneness causes people to express anger in destructive ways, and masculine shame-proneness causes men to express anger about sexual matters in a no less-destructive manner.

Masculine shame is toxic, and a man will go to great lengths to avoid it. Men fear failure at work, being wrong, showing fear, or appearing soft. In other words, the number one cause of shame in men is anything that might make them look weak. I know of one man who went to work every day for six months even though he didn't have a job. He desperately needed to avoid the mere appearance of failure. Another man took out a second mortgage on the family home without telling his wife so he could finance the upgrade of their kitchen and give her the impression that he was in a financially stronger position than he actually was. Both men felt too much shame to tell the truth to their wives about what was going on—they didn't want to run the risk of appearing weak.

Strongly influenced by the women's movement, Dr. Warren Farrell spent the first part of his career traveling around the country trying to convince men to be more like women based upon the popularity of his book *The Liberated Man*.[3] It took him more than a decade to notice that only women were coming to his lectures, and then he realized that women don't really want men to be like women, but they want men to pretend to be vulnerable anyway.[4] And again, what is the masculine response to these messages? Shame.

So what does masculine shame cause men to do? Well, mostly they get angry or shut down. They tell stories about the glory days in high school, use sports metaphors, and show open disdain for anything feminine. When anyone asks them how they feel, they respond with "fine," which stands for Feelings Inside Not Expressed. Masculine shame makes men feel they must do everything on their own, because if they can't, well, that will make them look weak.

However, feminine shame is no less toxic. Freud was completely wrong when he postulated that women have a weaker sense of morality because of defects in the superego (a conceptualization that no one holds today). As it turns out, women experience more shame and guilt than men do, and they are much more sensitive to transgressions and moral failings.[5] Women tend to have a stronger need to care for others than men do, and the moral decisions they make are based on this ethical imperative to nurture, whereas men are more likely to make ethical decisions based on their sense of justice.

As a result, women feel shame if they are not sympathetic to others, and they tend to take it personally when their relationships don't go well or are under attack. At the same time, women are supposed to be good at everything else they do, which easily gets interpreted as the requirement to be perfect. Feminine shame causes women to feel they are never enough at home, never enough at work, never enough for their husbands sexually, and never enough for their kids.[6] Being a bad mother (or failing to be one at all) is the second most shaming thing you could ever say to a woman. But sadly, even after all the decades of equal-rights movements, feminism, sensitivity training, and gender awareness raising that has been done, the number one source of shame for women centers on how they look. That's right: Not being pretty enough is still the greatest source of shame for women in America.[7] I know you are thinking that this idea is outdated and can't possibly still be true, but it is.

Feminine shame causes women to feel they are never enough, or always too much. It doesn't matter what their achievements are, or how hard they work at whatever it is they are doing. Everyone expects women to do it all, and of course, because no one can, women have no recourse but to feel shame. So women are supposed to be nice and sweet, but competent without having to make it look difficult. Because if a woman is too aggressive, well, she will be shamed for being unfeminine. Almost everyone knows the very common word for the hatred of women, *masochism*. But many people don't even know that the word for the hatred of men, *misandry*, even exists. Feminine shame appears to be built into the language of the culture itself, making it very difficult for women to escape it.

When it comes to intimate relationships between men and women, unresolved issues of shame are often at the core. Shame-prone partners are significantly more aggressive and destructive. Shame causes men to shut down and stonewall women, while it causes women to harshly criticize their men.[8] Shame is the enemy of vulnerability, and vulnerability is the only path to intimacy between men and women. If the healing of shame comes through courage, vulnerability, and acceptance, then the intimate relationship between a man and a women is a wonderful opportunity to heal a lifetime of previous sources of shame. Unfortunately, as you now know, shame makes us want to hide—the opposite of vulnerability. So you see the challenge for every intimate relationship. The very thing we need to do to heal our marriages of shame is the very thing none of us wants to do.

Godly guilt plays an important role in healthy interpersonal relationships between men and women.[9] Feeling bad when you hurt someone you love—and being motivated to make things right—is one of the crucial elements in making a marriage work. Marital therapy experts call this *making repairs*, and it is a sure sign that you are headed for a divorce if you lack the capacity to do this.[10]

This kind of shame-free guilt helps sex between a man and a woman be a bodily experience of a gift of love between them. But shame-proneness prevents this type of vulnerable concern for the other person, and sex then becomes a transactional experience where one person is trying to take something from the other one for their own personal pleasure. Shame and sex do not go well together. Shame causes us to become self-focused, and if you are afraid that your lack of worthiness is going to be exposed, then it is easy to use sex as something to hide behind. Sex was created by God to be the glue that holds a man and woman together in this difficult enterprise called marriage. Using it as a form of self-medication to numb your shame is not going to get you the intimacy it was designed to create.

The 100-billion-dollar pornography industry could be largely explained by masculine shame. Sexually shamed men fearing to appear weak might try to escape into the fantasy of having complete control by using the self-medicating effect of sexual pleasure to hide from their shame. At the same time, at least a portion of the 500-billion-dollar cosmetic industry could possibly be explained by feminine shame too. Women shamed by the impossible expectations to be the prettiest and most perfect woman in the room might try to hide from the shaming looks directed toward them behind the illusions that cosmetics can provide. Who could blame them for trying their best to appear to be what we all expect of them?

Because shame and sex do not go well together, some people make the error of acting like they have absolutely no shame at all when it comes to sex. But make no mistake about it: There is no such thing as shamelessness when it comes to sexuality. I know the entertainment industry and a good deal of romantic fiction would like you to believe that the most enjoyable form of sexual expression comes from the ability to shed all guilt and shame behind you, but this is not true.

What masquerades as shamelessness in any area, but especially when it comes to sexuality, has nothing to do with a lack of shame.

Acting with a brazen lack of concern for what others think of you is never an act of courage if it leads to a spiritual disconnection between you and others. In fact, shamelessness inevitably leads to depersonalization, which means you stop experiencing the one you are with as an actual person. If you treat people like objects, without any regard for their feelings, you will never deepen your connection with them. Instead, you will eventually experience others as things rather than people. And what happens then? You will suffer the breaking of the interpersonal bridge between you and others. In short, you will feel shame. If you ever see someone acting in a shameless manner, you will now understand the source of his or her behavior: shame.

So what should men and women do when it comes to their differences in the area of shame? The path to overcoming shame is still the same: courage, vulnerability, and acceptance. Even though women admit to feeling shame and guilt more often than men, it doesn't mean that they actually have more of a problem in these areas. Men feel guilt and shame too. They just have their feelings for different reasons, and they are less prone to speak about them.

So the first thing men and women need to do is to talk about their shame. That's right: acknowledge it—aloud. This takes courage and vulnerability. Women feel shame for their reasons, and men feel shame for theirs. Neither one is better nor worse. They are just different. And if we can talk about our feelings of shame with each other, and experience the acceptance of someone who doesn't feel shame the same way but still loves and accepts us anyway, well, that's a powerful source of healing for our shame.

You might think that the differences between men and women are obstacles to talking about our shame. But they are actually a sign of God's brilliance. You see, experiencing acceptance for the unacceptable heals shame. The fact that women cannot easily understand a man's reasons for feeling shame, and the fact that men have to stretch to grasp the reasons that a woman experiences hers, creates an even greater opportunity for grace.

I believe this is one of the reasons God made us so different. Feeling accepted when I feel unacceptable gives me the best idea of what it is like to be unconditionally loved. This is what God wants us all to experience. It was the reason he sent his Son. The apostle Paul made this pretty clear when he wrote, "God demonstrates his own love for us in this: While we were still sinners, Christ died for us" (Romans 5:8). Accepting someone who is just like me, or who deserves my acceptance, doesn't heal anything. But accepting someone who doesn't deserve it—that's grace. The grace of God heals us spiritually, and the grace we extend toward each other heals our shame. Because we are so different, it isn't easy for men and women to do it, but it is amazingly healing when we do.

APPENDIX:

Bible Verses on Shame, Shame-Free Living, and Guilt

BIBLE VERSES ON SHAME

Genesis 1:26

God said, "Let us make mankind in our image, in our likeness, so that they may rule over the fish in the sea and the birds in the sky, over the livestock and all the wild animals, and over all the creatures that move along the ground."

Genesis 1:31

God saw all that he had made, and it was very good.

Genesis 2:25

Adam and his wife were both naked, and they felt no shame.

Genesis 3:5-7

God knows that when you eat from it your eyes will be opened, and you will be like God, knowing good and evil. When the woman saw that the fruit of the tree was good for food and pleasing to the eye, and also desirable for gaining wisdom, she took some and ate it. She also gave some to her husband, who was with her, and he ate it. Then the eyes of both of them were opened, and they realized they were naked; so they sewed fig leaves together and made coverings for themselves.

Exodus 3:11

Moses said to God, "Who am I that I should go to Pharaoh and bring the Israelites out of Egypt?"

Exodus 33:19

The LORD said, "I will cause all my goodness to pass in front of you, and I will proclaim my name, the LORD, in your presence. I will have mercy on whom I will have mercy, and I will have compassion on whom I will have compassion."

Exodus 34:14

Do not worship any other god, for the LORD, whose name is Jealous, is a jealous God.

Psalm 4:2

How long will you people turn my glory into shame? How long will you love delusions and seek false gods?

Psalm 34:5

Those who look to him are radiant; their faces are never covered with shame.

Psalm 119:78

May the arrogant be put to shame for wronging me without cause; but I will meditate on your precepts.

Psalm 139:14

I praise you because I am fearfully and wonderfully made; your works are wonderful, I know that full well.

Proverbs 1:7

The fear of the LORD is the beginning of knowledge, but fools despise wisdom and instruction.

Proverbs 6:34

For jealousy arouses a husband's fury, and he will show no mercy when he takes revenge.

Proverbs 18:13

To answer before listening—that is folly and shame.

Proverbs 28:13

Whoever conceals their sins does not prosper, but the one who confesses and renounces them finds mercy.

Isaiah 6:5

"Woe to me!" I cried. "I am ruined! For I am a man of unclean lips, and I live among a people of unclean lips, and my eyes have seen the King, the Lord Almighty."

Isaiah 47:3

Your nakedness will be exposed and your shame uncovered.

Isaiah 61:7

Instead of your shame you will receive a double portion, and instead of disgrace you will rejoice in your inheritance. And so you will inherit a double portion in your land, and everlasting joy will be yours.

Zephaniah 3:19

At that time I will deal with all who oppressed you. I will rescue the lame; I will gather the exiles. I will give them praise and honor in every land where they have suffered shame.

Matthew 9:13

Go and learn what this means: "I desire mercy, not sacrifice." For I have not come to call the righteous, but sinners.

Matthew 10:29-30

Are not two sparrows sold for a penny? Yet not one of them will fall to the ground outside your Father's care. And even the very hairs of your head are all numbered.

Luke 14:11

All those who exalt themselves will be humbled, and those who humble themselves will be exalted.

Luke 18:13

The tax collector stood at a distance. He would not even look up to heaven, but beat his breast and said, "God, have mercy on me, a sinner."

John 1:14

The Word became flesh and made his dwelling among us. We have seen his glory, the glory of the one and only Son, who came from the Father, full of grace and truth.

John 1:17

The law was given through Moses; grace and truth came through Jesus Christ.

John 14:11

Believe me when I say that I am in the Father and the Father is in me.

John 15:5

I am the vine; you are the branches. If you remain in me and I in you, you will bear much fruit; apart from me you can do nothing.

Romans 1:26-27

Because of this, God gave them over to shameful lusts. Even their women exchanged natural sexual relations for unnatural ones.

Romans 5:5

Hope does not put us to shame, because God's love has been poured out into our hearts through the Holy Spirit, who has been given to us.

Romans 5:8

God demonstrates his own love for us in this: While we were still sinners, Christ died for us.

Romans 12:2-3

Do not conform to the pattern of this world, but be transformed by the renewing of your mind. Then you will be able to test and approve what God's will is—his good, pleasing and perfect will. For by the grace given me I say to every one of you: Do not think of yourself more highly than you ought, but rather think of yourself with sober judgment, in accordance with the faith God has distributed to each of you.

1 Corinthians 1:27

God chose the foolish things of the world to shame the wise; God chose the weak things of the world to shame the strong.

1 Corinthians 4:14

I am writing this not to shame you but to warn you as my dear children.

2 Corinthians 4:2

We have renounced secret and shameful ways; we do not use deception, nor do we distort the word of God. On the contrary, by setting forth the truth plainly we commend ourselves to everyone's conscience in the sight of God.

2 Corinthians 11:2

I am jealous for you with a godly jealousy. I promised you to one husband, to Christ, so that I might present you as a pure virgin to him.

Ephesians 5:12

It is shameful even to mention what the disobedient do in secret.

1 Timothy 1:13

Even though I was once a blasphemer and a persecutor and a violent man, I was shown mercy because I acted in ignorance and unbelief.

2 Timothy 1:12

That is why I am suffering as I am. Yet this is no cause for shame, because I know whom I have believed, and am convinced that he is able to guard what I have entrusted to him until that day.

Hebrews 2:7

You made them a little lower than the angels; you crowned them with glory and honor.

Hebrews 12:1-2

Let us run with perseverance the race marked out for us, fixing our eyes on Jesus, the pioneer and perfecter of faith. For the joy set before him he endured the cross, scorning its shame, and sat down at the right hand of the throne of God.

1 Peter 2:6

In Scripture it says: "See, I lay a stone in Zion, a chosen and precious cornerstone, and the one who trusts in him will never be put to shame."

1 Peter 3:4

Rather, it should be that of your inner self, the unfading beauty of a gentle and quiet spirit, which is of great worth in God's sight.

Jude 2

Mercy, peace and love be yours in abundance.

BIBLE VERSES ON SHAME-FREE LIVING

Job 5:2

Resentment kills a fool, and envy slays the simple.

Proverbs 11:2

When pride comes, then comes disgrace, but with humility comes wisdom.

Proverbs 14:30

A heart at peace gives life to the body, but envy rots the bones.

Proverbs 15:22

Plans fail for lack of counsel, but with many advisers they succeed.

Proverbs 16:24

Gracious words are a honeycomb, sweet to the soul and healing to the bones.

Proverbs 22:11

One who loves a pure heart and who speaks with grace will have the king for a friend.

Ecclesiastes 4:4

I saw that all toil and all achievement spring from one person's envy of another. This too is meaningless, a chasing after the wind.

Hosea 6:6

I desire mercy, not sacrifice, and acknowledgment of God rather than burnt offerings.

Micah 6:8

He has shown you, O mortal, what is good. And what does the LORD require of you? To act justly and to love mercy and to walk humbly with your God.

Zechariah 7:9

This is what the LORD Almighty said: "Administer true justice; show mercy and compassion to one another."

Matthew 5:7

Blessed are the merciful, for they will be shown mercy.

Matthew 5:39

If anyone slaps you on the right cheek, turn to them the other cheek also.

Matthew 6:1

Be careful not to practice your righteousness in front of others to be seen by them. If you do, you will have no reward from your Father in heaven.

Matthew 6:22

The eye is the lamp of the body. If your eyes are healthy, your whole body will be full of light.

Matthew 7:3

Why do you look at the speck of sawdust in your brother's eye and pay no attention to the plank in your own eye?

Matthew 10:8

Heal the sick, raise the dead, cleanse those who have leprosy, drive out demons. Freely you have received; freely give.

Matthew 16:25

Whoever wants to save their life will lose it, but whoever loses their life for me will find it.

Matthew 18:21-22

Peter came to Jesus and asked, "Lord, how many times shall I forgive my brother or sister who sins against me? Up to seven times?" Jesus answered, "I tell you, not seven times, but seventy-seven times."

Luke 6:37

Do not judge, and you will not be judged. Do not condemn, and you will not be condemned. Forgive, and you will be forgiven.

Luke 9:23

He said to them all: "Whoever wants to be my disciple must deny themselves and take up their cross daily and follow me."

Luke 23:34

Jesus said, "Father, forgive them, for they do not know what they are doing." And they divided up his clothes by casting lots.

John 3:8

The wind blows wherever it pleases. You hear its sound, but you cannot tell where it comes from or where it is going. So it is with everyone born of the Spirit.

John 13:14-15

Now that I, your Lord and Teacher, have washed your feet, you also should wash one another's feet. I have set you an example that you should do as I have done for you.

John 13:34

As I have loved you, so you must love one another.

Romans 12:8

If it is to encourage, then give encouragement; if it is giving, then give generously; if it is to lead, do it diligently; if it is to show mercy, do it cheerfully.

Romans 13:10

Love is the fulfillment of the law.

Romans 13:13

Let us behave decently, as in the daytime, not in carousing and drunkenness, not in sexual immorality and debauchery, not in dissension and jealousy.

Romans 14:20

All food is clean, but it is wrong for a person to eat anything that causes someone else to stumble.

1 Corinthians 13:4-7

Love is patient, love is kind. It does not envy, it does not boast, it is not proud. It does not dishonor others, it is not self-seeking, it is not easily angered, it keeps no record of wrongs. Love does not delight in evil but rejoices with the truth. It always protects, always trusts, always hopes, always perseveres.

Galatians 5:22-23

The fruit of the Spirit is love, joy, peace, forbearance, kindness, goodness, faithfulness, gentleness and self-control. Against such things there is no law.

Ephesians 4:26

In your anger do not sin: Do not let the sun go down while you are still angry.

Philippians 4:7

The peace of God, which transcends all understanding, will guard your hearts and your minds in Christ Jesus.

Colossians 2:18

Do not let anyone who delights in false humility and the worship of angels disqualify you. Such a person also goes into great detail about what they have seen; they are puffed up with idle notions by their unspiritual mind.

2 Timothy 1:7

The Spirit God gave us does not make us timid, but gives us power, love and self-discipline.

Hebrews 10:18

Where these have been forgiven, sacrifice for sin is no longer necessary.

James 1:19

My dear brothers and sisters, take note of this: Everyone should be quick to listen, slow to speak and slow to become angry.

James 2:13

Mercy triumphs over judgment.

James 3:13

Who is wise and understanding among you? Let them show it by their good life, by deeds done in the humility that comes from wisdom.

James 3:16

Where you have envy and selfish ambition, there you find disorder and every evil practice.

BIBLE VERSES ON GUILT

Psalm 38:4

My guilt has overwhelmed me like a burden too heavy to bear.

Mark 3:28

Truly I tell you, people can be forgiven all their sins and every slander they utter.

Mark 4:12

They may be ever seeing but never perceiving, and ever hearing but never understanding; otherwise they might turn and be forgiven!

Mark 11:25

When you stand praying, if you hold anything against anyone, forgive them, so that your Father in heaven may forgive you your sins.

Luke 7:47

I tell you, her many sins have been forgiven—as her great love has shown. But whoever has been forgiven little loves little.

Luke 17:3

So watch yourselves. If your brother or sister sins against you, rebuke them; and if they repent, forgive them.

John 9:41

Jesus said, "If you were blind, you would not be guilty of sin; but now that you claim you can see, your guilt remains."

Acts 20:32

Now I commit you to God and to the word of his grace, which can build you up and give you an inheritance among all those who are sanctified.

2 Corinthians 2:7

Now instead, you ought to forgive and comfort him, so that he will not be overwhelmed by excessive sorrow.

2 Corinthians 7:10-11

Godly sorrow brings repentance that leads to salvation and leaves no regret, but worldly sorrow brings death. See what this godly sorrow has produced in you: what earnestness, what eagerness to clear yourselves, what indignation, what alarm, what longing, what concern, what readiness to see justice done. At every point you have proved yourselves to be innocent in this matter.

Galatians 6:2

Carry each other's burdens, and in this way you will fulfill the law of Christ.

Colossians 3:13

Bear with each other and forgive one another if any of you has a grievance against someone. Forgive as the Lord forgave you.

Hebrews 10:22

Let us draw near to God with a sincere heart and with the full assurance that faith brings, having our hearts sprinkled to cleanse us from a guilty conscience and having our bodies washed with pure water.

James 5:16

Confess your sins to each other and pray for each other so that you may be healed. The prayer of a righteous person is powerful and effective.

1 John 1:9

If we confess our sins, he is faithful and just and will forgive us our sins and purify us from all unrighteousness.

Notes

CHAPTER 1: DO YOU HAVE A PROBLEM WITH GUILT OR SHAME?

1. A good book on this subject is *Not Just Friends* by Shirley Glass (New York: Free Press, 2003).

2. The first psychologist to make this distinction between guilt and shame was H.B. Lewis in *Shame and Guilt in Neurosis* (New York: International University Press, 1971).

3. Barbra Streisand and Andrew S. Karsch, *The Prince of Tides* (Culver City, CA: Columbia Pictures, 1991).

CHAPTER 2: WHAT CAUSES SHAME?

1. By the term *motivated*, I mean "moved to take action." *E-motions* motivate us to move in some direction.

2. Daniel Stern, *The Interpersonal World of the Infant* (New York: Basic Books, 1985).

3. Francis Broucek, *Shame and the Self* (New York: Guilford Press, 1991).

4. I am using the term *self* here in a very primitive sense. A developed sense of self versus others does not come online with great distinction until later, but we now know that infants have an emergent sense of self from birth and are organizing their affective experiences into some level of meaning.

5. Gershen Kaufman, *Shame: The Power of Caring* (Cambridge, MA: Schenkman, 1890).

6. Louis Smedes, *Shame and Grace: Healing the Shame We Don't Deserve* (San Francisco: HarperSanFrancisco, 1993).

7. I have spoken with Greg a few times in person. You can see a video of his testimony at www.brooklyntabernacle.org.

8. The technical term for these unconscious beliefs is *organizing principles*, and you can find out more about them by reading Robert Stolorow and George Atwood, *Contexts of Being: The Intersubjective Foundations of Psychological Life* (Hillsdale, NJ: Analytic Press, 1992).

9. June Tangney and Ronda Dearing, *Shame and Guilt* (New York: Guilford Press, 2002).

10. James 1:19-20 warns us to be "slow to anger" because if we are not careful, we will not use anger in the way God created it to be used. Anger does serve a godly purpose if used wisely.

11. June Tangney, Jeffery Stuewig, and Andres Martinez, "The Two Faces of Shame: The Roles of Shame and Guilt in Predicting Recidivism," *Psychological Science* 25 (March 2014): 799-805.

12. Antonio Damasio, *Descartes' Error: Emotion, Reason, and the Human Brain* (New York: Avon, 1994).

13. Brené Brown, *Daring Greatly: How the Courage to Be Vulnerable Transforms the Way to Live, Love, Parent, and Lead* (New York: Avery, 2015).

14. John Bradshaw, *Healing the Shame That Binds You* (Deerfield Beach, FL: Health Communications, 1988).

CHAPTER 3: THE POWER OF VULNERABILITY

1. Brené Brown, *Daring Greatly: How the Courage to Be Vulnerable Transforms the Way We Live, Love, Parent, and Lead* (New York: Avery, 2015).

2. D.W. Winnicott, *The Maturational Processes and the Facilitating Environment: Studies in the Theory of Emotional Development* (New York: International Universities Press, 1965), 37-55.

3. This philosophy was made famous by psychologist Fritz Perls, who adapted it from a poem by Henry Wadsworth Longfellow.

4. Alan Schore, *Affect Regulation and the Origin of the Self* (Hillsdale, NJ: Lawrence Erlbaum Associates, 1994).

5. Robert Stolorow and George Atwood, *Contexts of Being: The Intersubjective Foundations of Psychological Life* (Hillsdale, NJ: Analytic Press, 1992), 7-28.

6. My colleague Carmen Berry and I have written an entire book on this subject titled *Who's to Blame: Escape the Victim Trap and Gain Personal Power in Your Relationships* (Colorado Springs: NavPress, 1996).

7. Brown, *Daring Greatly*, 199.

CHAPTER 4: HUMILITY HAS NOTHING TO DO WITH HUMILIATION

1. Susan M. Johnson, *The Practice of Emotionally Focused Marital Therapy: Creating Connection* (New York: Brunner/Mazel, 1996).

2. Sue Johnson with Kenneth Sanderfer, *Created for Connection: The "Hold Me Tight" Guide for Christian Couples* (New York: Little, Brown, 2016), Kindle edition, 7.

3. I have the honor of having Dr. Susan Johnson's permission to tell her story (personal communication, November 17, 2016).

4. Johnson, *Created for Connection*, Kindle edition, 4.

5. Johnson, *Created for Connection*, Kindle edition, 6.

6. June Tangney and Ronda Dearing, *Shame and Guilt* (New York: Guilford Press, 2002), 44.

CHAPTER 5: JESUS AND SELF-ESTEEM

1. Daniel Stern, *The Interpersonal World of the Infant* (New York: Basic Books, 1985).

2. V. Gallese, M.N. Eagle, and P. Migone, "Intentional Attunement: Mirror Neurons and the Neural Underpinnings of Interpersonal Relations," *Journal of the American Psychoanalytic Association* 55, no. 1 (Winter 2007): 131-76.

3. E. Tronick, L.B. Adamson, H. Als, and T.B. Brazelton, "Infant Emotions in Normal and Pertubated Interactions," Paper presented at the biennial meeting of the Society for Research in Child Development, Denver, CO, April 1975.

4. For a good discussion of this, see Curt Thompson, *The Soul of Shame: Retelling the Stories We Believe About Ourselves* (Downers Grove, IL: IVP Books, 2015), Kindle edition.

5. Ibid., loc. 2688 of 3248.

6. This quote is generally attributed to Albert Einstein, but scholars don't all agree on this.

7. Bernard Brandchaft, "Systems of Pathological Accommodation and Change in Analysis," *Psychoanalytic Psychology* 24, no. 4 (2007): 667-87.

CHAPTER 6: RESENTMENT: THE DEADLY WEAPON THAT BACKFIRES

1. I am indebted to the influence of Jeffrie Murphy and Jean Hampton's book *Forgiveness and Mercy* (Cambridge: Cambridge University Press, 1988) and their many legal concepts surrounding forgiveness gleaned from their years of law practice.

CHAPTER 7: HOW TO HEAL ENVY AND JEALOUSY

1. Jonathan Haidt made this metaphor popular in *The Happiness Hypothesis* (New York: Basic Books, 2006).

2. Although, if you look into it, you will find that criminals accused of crimes of passion have displayed a long history of impulse control problems and pathology. Thinking of a jealous rage as a single outburst of jealousy that doesn't have a history to explain it is not really accurate.

CHAPTER 8: THE SECRET CAUSE NARCISSISM

1. Richard Gramzow and June Tangney, "Proneness to Shame and the Narcissistic Personality," *Personality and Social Psychology Bulletin* 18, no. 3 (1992): 369-76.

2. The classic psychoanalytic book here is Andrew Morrison, *Shame: The Underside of Narcissism* (Hillsdale, NJ: Analytic Press, 1989).

3. June Tangney and Jeffrey Stuewig, "Shame, Guilt, and Remorse: Implications for Offender Populations," *Journal of Forensic Psychiatry and Psychology* 22, no. 5 (September 1, 2011): 706-23.

4. Byron Johnson, *More God, Less Crime: Why Faith Matters and How It Could Matter More* (West Conshohocken, PA: Templeton, 2011).

CHAPTER 9: THE DIFFERENT FACES OF SHAME

1. Rhonda Fee and June Tangney, "Procrastination: A Means of Avoiding Shame or Guilt?" *Journal of Social Behavior and Personality* 5, no. 5 (June 2012): 167-84.

2. Mark Baker, *Jesus, the Greatest Therapist Who Ever Lived* (San Francisco: HarperOne, 2007), 131.

3. Charles Strozier, David Terman, and James Jones, *The Fundamentalist Mindset: Psychological Perspectives on Religion, Violence, and History* (New York: Oxford University Press, 2010).

4. Brené Brown, *Daring Greatly: How the Courage to Be Vulnerable Transforms the Way to Live, Love, Parent, and Lead* (New York: Penguin, 2012), Kindle edition, 177.

CHAPTER 10: WHAT'S THE POINT OF THERAPY?

1. Bruce D. Perry and Maia Szalavitz, *Born for Love: Why Empathy Is Essential—and Endangered* (New York: HarperCollins, 2010).

2. June Tangney and Ronda Dearing, *Shame and Guilt* (New York: Guilford Press, 2002).

3. The apostle Paul tried to clarify this to a group of philosophers in Athens when he explained, "For in him we live and move and have our being" (Acts 17:28). He was quoting one of their own poets in an attempt to help them see that worshipping idols doesn't make any sense if God is spirit and "we are his offspring" (verse 28) as some of them already believed. Human beings are fundamentally relational and cannot exist as isolated islands. When we try, we end up living as something less than human. God is not "out there" to be worshipped from afar; he is already here, ready to live in us if we are ready to acknowledge our relationship with him. There is no "inside" and "outside" of the human mind; there is only acknowledgment of relationship or not.

CHAPTER 11: OVERCOMING SHAME

1. Louis Smedes, *Shame and Grace: Healing the Shame We Don't Deserve* (San Francisco: HarperSanFrancisco, 1993), 161.

2. See these books by Brené Brown: *Rising Strong: How the Ability to Rest Transforms the Way We Live, Love, and Lead* (New York: Random House, 2017); *The Gifts of Imperfection: Let Go of Who You Think You're Supposed to Be and Embrace Who You Are* (Century City, MN: Hazelton, 2010); and *I Thought It Was Just Me (But It Isn't): Making the Journey from "What Will People Think?" to "I Am Enough"* (New York: Penguin, 2007).

3. Brené Brown, *Daring Greatly: How the Courage to Be Vulnerable Transforms the Way to Live, Love, Parent, and Lead* (New York: Avery, 2015), 80.

4. Smedes, *Shame and Grace*, 105.

5. The most brilliant supervisor I ever had, Dr. Robert Stolorow, referred to clinicians as *practical philosophers*. We are helping our patients make meaning out of their lives. As a Christian, I prefer the term *practical theologian*.

6. I am paraphrasing Dr. Smedes here from Smedes, *Shame and Grace*, 119.

7. See Luke 7:50; 2 Corinthians 1:6; Philippians 2:12; Matthew 24:13; Romans 13:11.

Afterword: The Differences Between Men and Women

1. June Price Tangney and Ronda L. Dearing, *Shame and Guilt* (New York: Guilford Press, 2002).

2. Brené Brown, *Daring Greatly: How the Courage to Be Vulnerable Transforms the Way We Live, Love, Parent, and Lead* (New York: Avery, 2015).

3. Warren Farrell, *The Liberated Man: Beyond Masculinity: Freeing Men and Their Relationships with Women* (New York: Random House, 1974).

4. Warren Farrell, *Why Men Are the Way They Are* (New York: McGraw-Hill, 1986).

5. June Price Tangney and Ronda L. Dearing, "Gender Differences in Morality," in Robert F. Bornstein and Joseph M. Masling, *The Psychodynamics of Gender and Gender Role* (Washington, DC: American Psychological Association, 2002), 251-69, http://dx.doi.org/10.1037/10450-007.

6. Brown, *Daring Greatly*, 87.

7. Brown, *Daring Greatly*. 86.

8. John Gottman and Nan Silver, *The Seven Principles for Making Marriage Work: A Practical Guide from the Country's Foremost Relationship Expert* (New York: Three Rivers Press, 1999).

9. 2 Corinthians 7:10-11.

10. Gottman and Silver, *The Seven Principles for Making Marriage Work*.

To learn more about Harvest House books and
to read sample chapters, visit our website:

www.harvesthousepublishers.com

HARVEST HOUSE PUBLISHERS
EUGENE, OREGON